Dear Peggy —

Hope you enjoy

Jim Smith

— look up the b. long

Outside the Gate

The Inspiring True Story of an Orphaned Girl Who Survived the Abusive Canadian Foster System

JUNE SMITH

Cover Design By Adam Del Monte
Illustrations by Amanda Lagerquist

Copyright © 2022 June Smith.

All rights reserved. No part of this book may be used or reproduced by any means, graphic, electronic, or mechanical, including photocopying, recording, taping or by any information storage retrieval system without the written permission of the author except in the case of brief quotations embodied in critical articles and reviews.

This book is a work of non-fiction. Unless otherwise noted, the author and the publisher make no explicit guarantees as to the accuracy of the information contained in this book and in some cases, names of people and places have been altered to protect their privacy.

WestBow Press books may be ordered through booksellers or by contacting:

WestBow Press
A Division of Thomas Nelson & Zondervan
1663 Liberty Drive
Bloomington, IN 47403
www.westbowpress.com
844-714-3454

Because of the dynamic nature of the Internet, any web addresses or links contained in this book may have changed since publication and may no longer be valid. The views expressed in this work are solely those of the author and do not necessarily reflect the views of the publisher, and the publisher hereby disclaims any responsibility for them.

Any people depicted in stock imagery provided by Getty Images are models, and such images are being used for illustrative purposes only. Certain stock imagery © Getty Images.

Cover Design By Adam Del Monte
Illustrations by Amanda Lagerquist

Scripture quotations marked NIV are taken from The Holy Bible, New International Version®, NIV® Copyright © 1973, 1978, 1984, 2011 by Biblica, Inc.® Used by permission. All rights reserved worldwide.

ISBN: 978-1-6642-6802-9 (sc)
ISBN: 978-1-6642-6803-6 (e)

Library of Congress Control Number: 2022910199

Print information available on the last page.

WestBow Press rev. date: 07/23/2022

The Children of the Dance

This is not a misery story
It is a voice for change
It is a voice raised
In the music of the dance
For the children ahead
In the memory of the children dead
They are the children of the dance
They are the wounded children
Healed and alive
May they dance in freedom
Without shame
Without pain
The children of the dance

/j.smith

Throughout the world, through no fault of their own, children are rejected and isolated, living outside the gate of society.

This story is dedicated to those children.

The story I write is a true story, although I used creative license in the dialogue; I cannot recall whole conversations. However, each incident shown is true. My story is historical, but as my research has shown, it is also a current story.

Outside the Gate is dedicated to my brother Freddie and to my own beautiful children I have been blessed with.

Contents

Chapter 1	A New Name	1
Chapter 2	The Oasis	7
Chapter 3	The Hiding Place	12
Chapter 4	Forbidden Fruit	20
Chapter 5	Candies and Love	27
Chapter 6	The Farm	32
Chapter 7	Being a Girl	42
Chapter 8	The Bird Leaves the Nest	43
Chapter 9	A New Home	46
Chapter 10	The Tea Party	54
Chapter 11	Consequences	67
Chapter 12	A Spoonful of Sugar	74
Chapter 13	The Years of the Locusts	79
Chapter 14	The Escape	95
Chapter 15	The Run	99
Chapter 16	A World without Pity	107
Chapter 17	The Delinquent	115
Chapter 18	Broken Wings	120
Chapter 19	Birds in a Cage	131
Chapter 20	Do No Harm	138
Chapter 21	Girls Living under the Shadows	145

Chapter 22	Between the Devil and the Deep	150
Chapter 23	The Cell	153
Chapter 24	The Rope	159
Chapter 25	Released from the Snare	166
Chapter 26	Bird in Flight	173
Chapter 27	A Safe Place	179
Chapter 28	Looking for Answers	186
Chapter 29	Strange Things Indeed	194

Appendix 201
Acknowledgments 205
Epilogue 207

Chapter 1
A NEW NAME

> Victory has a thousand fathers, but defeat is an orphan.
> —John F. Kennedy

Sometimes, every choice is the wrong choice.

Should two small children be pulled out of danger when to do so would also place them in danger?

In a dark, cold basement apartment in Toronto, my brother and I slept and tried to keep warm. It was in the early morning hours, and the sun had not risen. Freddie was six, and I was four years old, and as so often happened, we were alone as we huddled together trying to keep ourselves warm in the darkness of the cold room.

The small basement window was partially covered with built-up snow and ice; it had become frozen open, allowing the freezing air to blow into the room where we slept.

Something woke us up, and Freddie got out of our bed and turned on the light in the kitchen. I followed closely behind him, like his shadow. The soft light of early morning was beginning to cast shadows in the room.

Freddie opened the fridge, and we peered in, hungrily looking for food. The fridge was empty other than two lonely bottles of beer.

Freddie managed to open one, and in our desperation, we tried drinking it, but found it disgusting and spit it out. We hated the smell.

Stacks of dirty dishes covered the counters and filled the sink. Rodent droppings were scattered throughout the apartment on the floor and inside the cupboards.

Bugs crawled around the congealed food on the dirty dishes. Freddie and I had often amused each other by trying to catch the bugs and see who could kill the most.

We meticulously counted their dead bodies. Once when I was hungry, I tried eating a few. Freddie yelled at me and forced me to bring them up.

When he put the light on that morning, we could see small dark creatures scurry into the corners of the kitchen. Freddie would grab a broom and run at them to scare them back into whatever dark hole they had come from. Unwelcome visitors. I shuddered.

Perhaps nibbling at our feet in the night?

I thought I had felt something that night and wondered if they had caused us to wake up. The thought made me shiver with horror.

I hoped they would not bite us when we slept because some of those shadows looked large to me.

Freddie said, "They are rats."

"Do they bite?"

Freddie just looked at me and shrugged his shoulders.

That was scary.

Refuse covered the floor. It was hard to avoid sharp objects that hurt our feet. Neither one of us had slippers, so we started to wear shoes in the apartment to prevent injury. Sometimes we kept our shoes on when we slept.

The appliances were also covered with grime and grease and now looked yellow. The apartment smelled of unwashed bodies, old cigarette smoke, and stale alcohol.

The washroom stank of urine and excrement. This mingling of smells created their own symphony of unbreathable air. We had no idea how to overcome this unpleasantness, so we just lived with it.

The sheets on our bed had lost their original color and were covered with dirt. We kept trying to smooth them out but lost that battle and ended up wrapping ourselves in them, along with a ratty old blanket on the bed.

As unpleasant as all this was, it was still our home. We had become resigned to the reality of our life. We had each other.

The big cat that shared the basement with us did not come into our space, as it was too cold for her.

Freddie and I loved the cat, but she did not love us, as we often stole her food that was left downstairs by the property owner, so she hissed at us when we approached.

She was a lovely tabby cat, and her job was to kill the mice and rats, but our place was too cold for her. She had wisely found a spot near the furnace. The rats stayed with us, along with the mice and whatever else that was attracted to filth.

That night, the cold overcame our hunger, and once again, as we had several times before, we crept out of our apartment and went into the furnace room. We were not supposed to, but we were driven by cold.

We spotted the cat sleeping in her corner, and she raised her head at us and stared. We saw her eyes glinting in the darkness; they flashed a warning to us.

We were afraid of her and felt guilty for stealing her food. Hunger had transformed us into little animals. Her cat food tasted good to us.

We did not gag on it; we were glad of it. We hurriedly grabbed some and stuffed it in our mouths. That cat knew we were the culprits, and we saw anger in her eyes.

As we crept into the furnace room, we were quiet as we remembered our mother's warning.

"Keep quiet, and stay put until I get home," she said, "or they will throw us out on the street, and they will take you away."

We did not know who they were, but in our minds, the way she referred to them made us think they would hurt us. They became our monsters under our bed.

Shivering in the darkness, we opened the door to the old coal furnace and threw paper on the fire. Soon the basement filled with smoke, and the landlord came thundering down the stairs and pulled us outside.

Fire trucks and cars with flashing lights surrounded the house.

The memories of my life began there, as the years before disappeared from my mind. I still know that one person played with me. One person held me when we huddled together in the night. One person heard my cries. My brother Freddie was that person.

That morning, child welfare workers appeared and took us away, and soon we were pulled apart. That began the separation from my brother. We did not hug each other goodbye, as we did not know we would be separated that morning.

We found out who they were.

Although we were separated, I did not forget him, and today, when I think of Freddie, my heart is sad. I have a shadowy picture in my mind of a little boy who comforted me in the night.

I visualize him walking away and slowly disappearing from me, waving back at me. It is how I imagine our goodbye, as I knew he would never have left me willingly, just as I hated to leave him. He disappeared in a fog of time.

In my heart, I did not say goodbye.

Predators waited in the darkness for us. Far worse than hunger and cold and dirty dishes in our motherless flat. Larger and darker than the rats that roamed our apartment that night.

June, age three, and Freddie, age five, with their mother near Gravenhurst, Ontario.

June at age four, after she was separated
from her brother, Freddie.

Chapter 2
THE OASIS

> The quality of Mercy is not strained
> It droppeth
> as the gentle rain from heaven
> In the place beneath it is twice blessed.
> It blesses him that gives and him that takes.
>
> —William Shakespeare, *The Merchant of Venice*

"Too many mommies and daddies."

That was my cry in the first year after my separation from my family. Five years old and still bewildered. Trauma and grief blocked the year out. Files I have been able to obtain describe a lost little girl. Emotionally distraught, I cried, and my moods went from excited to withdrawn. I was now a ward of the state and under the care of Canada's Child Welfare. I became aware who *they* were.

I had been shunted around from place to place in the first year. This happened too many times, from the age of four to five years of age.

At night, I would cry out with terrors, and in the day, I would wander off, looking for my brother and my mother. My heart was broken, not comprehending why my mother and my brother were gone. I kept asking, but no one could answer me.

Testing was done by the Toronto Psychiatric Hospital, and it was determined I needed help to adjust to my loss prior to being fostered.

At five years of age, I entered an orphanage in Toronto.

"Strawberry Fields Forever," the song John Lennon wrote, was drawn from his experience as a boy, climbing in the large trees outside the Salvation Army orphanage in Liverpool, England. The Nest was the fond name given to these orphanages which were situated around the world.

The Nest in Toronto was founded on January 15, 1941, after the Salvation Army purchased a large estate from a relative of John Taylor; it was located on Broadview Avenue, close to Danforth Avenue. The seventy-five-year-old home had twenty-one rooms and was large enough for thirty-five girls. It was surrounded by beautiful chestnut and apple trees along the border of the property.

The day I arrived, a young woman named Miss Julie welcomed me and showed me around.

I was glad I did not have to call her Mom and could call her Miss Julie, instead. I did not want another Mom. I had one mother, and she was coming back for me soon.

I'm only here for a little while, I comforted myself. Soon my mother and Freddie and I would be back together again. I made up stories to myself to explain our separation because I did not know why they were gone. I lived with the expectation of them walking back into my life soon. Every day, the circle of hope and disappointment was repeated.

Are they coming back today?

I would wake up with that question and often fall asleep in tears of disappointment. Round and round the circle went, that relentless grief. My love did not disappear, and neither did my grief.

It was with that grief still alive in me that I arrived at the orphanage.

When I met Miss Julie, she said, "Hi, June. Let's go upstairs, and I will show you your bedroom."

She picked up my small bag of clothes and held my hand as we went up the stairs.

I was astonished at the large estate.

The Victorian home had winding stairs and wide rails. I imagined sliding down them would be fun. When we got to the top of the stairs, I looked down and had second thoughts. The stairs were full of girls running up and down and skirting around us. The estate was immense to me; I looked up, and the sounds of the girls were magnified by the lofty ceiling. Voices of little girls bounced off the walls, filling the house. Everything was new and different, and I felt afraid. Hearing the girls laughing and chattering eased my fear.

The aroma of cooking food drifted up. The combination of girls squealing and having fun and the enticing smell of food created a feeling of relief and reduced my anxiety.

Somewhere in the distance, the soft notes of a piano drifted up. I felt something stirring in me. I looked around and felt new sensations; I glanced up at Miss Julie frequently. My anxiety and the butterflies in my stomach were settling, but I wanted to know everything was okay. Miss Julie would look down and smile at me. This was a balm to my fear.

We stopped briefly at a large washroom, which held rows of sinks and bathtubs, and then we carried on to the bedrooms down the hall.

Miss Julie held my hand while we walked. She gently guided me around, bending down to point things out. She continued to look down at me and smile.

She seems nice, I thought.

Strangers came and went, but they did not stay. I would be told how pretty I was. It did not matter if I was pretty because they still left.

Would she stay?

She guided me back down the winding stairs to the main floor. We peeked into the kitchen, where the smells were coming from. Then we continued to a great room. In one corner of the room, I saw the source of the music I had heard. A young woman was playing the piano, and little girls gathered around her. They were singing songs I did not know. I enjoyed listening to them. They sounded like happy songs. Miss Julie and I stood there silently for a few moments. I was quiet, trying to absorb this new experience and take it all in.

Is this place safe? I wondered.

Miss Julie reached down and ruffled my hair.

"This is where we watch movies," she said. "Have you seen the Little Rascals?"

"No," I said.

"They are a gang of kids. They will make you laugh.

She leaned down to me when she spoke. Her eyes twinkled, and I thought she liked those movies too.

This was my introduction to the orphanage; as the days rolled by, I settled in. The schedule of the orphanage and the routine were comforting.

Meals were regular, and in the dining room, the staff sat at the front of a long table, and the girls sat at smaller tables. Our tables were close to each other.

The girls would crawl under the table and tickle each other's feet. We would also trade food. Little girls, full of fun. We made a lot of noise in that room, giggling and laughing with sounds of clinking dishes. There were many spills.

I hated lima beans, but another girl loved them, so she would give me her beets, which she hated, and I would give her my beans.

We always had full bellies at the orphanage, and we got snacks after school.

In inclement weather, we'd run downstairs with a cookie in our hands to play in the big playroom in the basement.

The Victorian house vibrated with the noise of kids. Music was a part of the sounds. We loved to sing, and there was often someone at the piano. The Salvation Army Band would visit us, and then we would hear trumpets. My favorite time was Sundays in the great room with Bible stories and music.

The small chores we were given were not hard. We would take turns helping with the cleanup after meals and drying the dishes.

At night, we went to sleep with warm milk and cookies in our bellies. Hunger faded from my memory.

In the night, lying in my bed with my eyes closed, I heard one of the women quietly approach my bed. I opened my eyes like slits and pretended I was asleep. She said a soft prayer over me and whispered my name in the prayer and then gently turned me and rearranged the blankets back over me.

"If you feel us turning you over," she explained, "it is because lying in one position too long is bad for your heart."

The nights for me now became full of angels rather than the demons I had been fighting. I felt those women walking with the soft glow of the lights in their hands were really angels visiting me in the night. Their whispered prayer made the demons slither away.

This was new, and I soaked it up. In my memory, every woman at the orphanage was a Miss Julie. I started to become attached to them. I did not call them Mom, but they began to assume that role in my life. For a while, a brief time, the women and the girls in the orphanage became my family.

When Miss Julie gave me a hug, she would often sweep me up in her arms and hum a soft little song, and the hug would stretch longer as she held me and rocked me gently in her arms.

Leaning my head on her shoulder, I would tease her by trying to undo her hair, which was swept in a bun, and then we would make a game of it.

I enjoyed pulling out the pins that held her hair up and watching it fall. When she allowed me to do that, her hair was lovely and soft as I ran my fingers through it.

I was astonished at the length of it as it fell down her back in beautiful waves. She would laughingly shake it loose and wrap it back up and twirl it into her bun with ease.

Both of us would end up laughing in delight, enjoying the moment, and enjoying each other.

I wanted to remain a bird in the Nest.

Chapter 3

THE HIDING PLACE

"This is yours, and no one is allowed to open it but you," said Miss Julie.

Shortly after my arrival, Miss Julie took me down to the playroom and walked me over to a box sitting in the middle of the large room in the basement. Running over, I stopped in front of it. In the center of the room, it took a principal place.

Miss Julie came over and joined me.

"Lift the lid."

Lifting the lid, I saw my name. Someone had designed the inside of the lid with little hearts and flowers. Seeing my own name filled me with happiness. With pleasure, I saw that my initials were on the outside of the box near the keyhole. Miss Julie pointed that out to me.

Handing me a key, she showed me how to close and lock the

box. Grasping the key in my hand, I tried it a few times before I got it right. My hands felt clumsy, and with Miss Julie's eyes on me, my mind froze. When I tried to turn the key, my hands shook.

She stood silently, and I sensed her cheering me on. She made soft noises of encouragement. I was ready to give up when after several attempts, I finally turned the key.

Yes, it worked. Closing and opening the lid of the toy box absorbed me for a few minutes while Miss Julie waited. I peeked inside and was delighted to see treasures: books, pencils, paper, and crayons.

"You can keep your toys in there and your own private notes or anything special you want. You can print your name on the inside of the books."

I immediately pulled out a book. She handed me a pen, and I printed my name slowly and carefully on the inside of the book.

"No one will go there, and the contents of this toy box will always be yours."

The box was big enough for me to climb inside.

I looked up at her with surprise; she repeated her words and nodded at me.

"It is yours. It belongs to you. It is your private place."

Inside was a jewelry box. When I opened the lid, a miniature ballet dancer swirled around with tinkling sounds of music.

The toy box became my own special possession. Later, I would hoard candies and treats in there and keep the notes I wrote to my bother. I drew red hearts all over them and dreamed that I would be able to give them to Freddie. My box of dreams. I tucked the notes into the bottom of the toy box and placed them in an envelope that Miss Julie gave me.

The box was big, and I was tiny. When I bent over to forage, I was halfway inside of it. I soon learned I could climb right in.

I would hide in the box and close the lid over myself. Darkness enveloped me, and noises became dulled. I did not mind that. When I closed the lid, I was there with my treasures and Freddie. I would talk to him in there and tell him all my secrets and pretend I was with him again. He would love the notes and hearts I made for him.

Sometimes, I would fall asleep in that toy box with all my imaginations and dreams. Miss Julie would know where to find me. I would hear her tap on the lid, and I'd push it open and climb back out.

The toy boxes were fun. Every girl had one. On wintry days, we girls would climb into our boxes and talk to each other with our heads popping up and down.

We sang to each other, singing lustily and then breaking out into giggles because we would forget the words and start making up our own songs, popping up and down in tune to our own music. Often, we would sing Sunday school songs:

> Precious jewels, precious jewels, they
> will shine in their beauty
> Bright gems for his crown.
>
> —William Cushing

We liked that song, as Miss Julie told us we were the precious jewels.

Black squares were painted on the floor of the playroom, and we sang nursery rhymes as we hopped onto and off the squares. Our voices filled the room with sweet, melodic sounds of little girls' voices, children making music and dancing and skipping among the squares. We made up our own songs and our own dances. The sounds are still there in my mind. We bounced balls back and forth and skipped rope there in the winter.

We were sisters for a while and tried to stick together as much as possible. We had heard a girl had gone missing in the ravine near the orphanage, so we walked together holding each other's hands in a line. We feared that ravine. There were monsters down there.

At the school, we were seldom bullied.

If someone tried, we would call on the older girls. Instead, we were another curiosity, like the woman who frequently appeared at recess, wearing grotesque makeup, and ranting in the schoolyard. She wore a big shawl and carried a cat. We crowded around, fascinated. We knew she was harmless, but she would stand before the kids and give rousing speeches.

She stood up on some sort of platform, and the kids gathered around her. We did not understand what she was saying, but her voice was loud, and she waved her hands around.

As an orphan, I drew attention. The older kids at school would give me pennies and treats to bribe me to sing for them.

I would sing as they gathered around me at recess, as we huddled together in the corner of the school building. I loved to mimic Shirley Temple. They would make requests for me to sing songs they wanted to hear.

"Baby face, you've got the cutest little baby face," was one I sang for them.

They were nosy about me. Real orphans in person were different from the ones they had read about in books. I was not a little Annie. The whole subject fascinated them. Not me.

"Are you an orphan?"

"What happened to your mom and dad?"

I would make up stories that they were coming back or that they had been kidnapped. I made up every kind of story because I really did not understand myself.

I hated it when they asked me those questions because I did not know what to tell them. The grief I was trying to hide and the desperation to not be different would be brought to the surface.

My family was in my heart, and although my separation had happened, they were still my family. I hated being called an orphan and doubly hated the word *ward*. Names wanted to stick to me, and in my mind, I wanted to unstick them. Especially when the names brought stigma with them. No one explained why the words made me sad. Feeling "less than," I wanted to be the same, not less.

I tried to convince them and myself that I had a family, but I was in an orphanage, so they did not believe me. When they were curious, I ignored the questions most of the time, but I often made-up stories. I wanted to be normal. The orphanage tried to include normal activities in our lives. The events that kids do, they did with us.

Trick-or-treating at Halloween was a challenge for thirty little girls.

However, we still went out; it was done with great care, with groups of six girls with one adult with each group, sticking together and going around the streets near the orphanage. We dressed up in Disney character costumes such as Bugs Bunny or Snow White. Nothing too scary. We were scared enough.

I could see the family inside handing out the candies and would be jealous of that, wishing I could experience that, as I looked in wonder at the warm scene.

What would it be like living in one of those homes? I wondered.

When my thoughts went that way, I would feel sad. In the middle of fun, I would push the feelings away, but they still intruded. They stayed with me at school when I heard the other children talking about their lives. Longing filled my heart.

Christmas came to the orphanage. We helped decorate a huge Christmas tree on the main floor. The tree was at the base of the winding stairs.

We made some of the decorations ourselves, cutting circles of different colored paper, taping them together, and hanging them on the tree.

The young women at the orphanage were efficient, but some of my creations were a little crooked and had to be fixed. Miss Julie sat by my side and helped me. When I did manage to make one work, I would be excited.

"Look at this one," I said proudly, holding up a chain I managed to make.

"Go ahead, put it on the tree," Miss Julie said.

Delighted, I would run over to the tree and hang up my chain, full of tape, and crooked, but I was proud of it, even though it took forever to make. That just added to the fun.

We held our finished products up proudly to each other. The little plastic scissors were difficult for me to manage, as my fingers became thumbs. Miss Julie was patient as she helped me. Learning for me was always better in private. I was afraid of a slap. An audience caused my mind to go blank, and my clumsiness intensified.

The old Victorian estate was a perfect setting for a Christmas wonderland. When snow hit some of the windows, the scene became magical. I would stand in front of the tree when it was lit up, getting lost in the wonder of it. This was my first experience of a real Christmas. The snow falling outside, and the lights and music, created magic for me.

Smells coming from the big old kitchen filled the house with comfort. There was a wonderful cook who created special cookies for us. The house was full of good smells. Tables were set up for us, and we decorated them. We could not resist the temptation to try some.

The voices of the other girls playing faded in that magical world of Christmas; I was transfixed with wonder at all the sights and smells, lost in my dream world.

Time stood still as I stood staring at the mammoth Christmas tree at the bottom of the stairs. In a little while, Miss Julie would tap me on the head in the gentle way that only she could do, rousing me from my daydreams and telling me that treats were waiting for me and warm chocolate milk. The other girls and I would gather around the table set up for us in the great room.

Christmas music surrounded us. We sang the old carols by the piano. Moved by the music and the special time, we sang with our whole hearts.

The young women knew the carols and sang the words. We joined in and watched their mouths, following their lead. Miss Julie sang one that remained with me until I heard it again many years later. The haunting music resonated with me.

> In the bleak midwinter, frosty wind made moan.
> Earth stood hard as iron, water as a stone.
>
> (Christina Rossetti)

Years later, I would hear that old carol and wonder at the unlikely place the song would trigger the memory of where I had heard it and when. It took me back to the time when I was six years old at the Salvation Army orphanage, remembering the sweet sound of Miss Julie singing.

Miss Julie started to sing the carol as a solo because no one else knew it. She sat at the piano with her beautiful hair flowing down her back. Her sweet voice rose in the room, and the high ceiling created a strong echo floating down to us. This made the night magical. I stood in awe, carried away by the music. All of us girls were silent, listening to her.

After our treats, the girls and I would sit and hear the story of Christmas. We were already dressed in our nighties and housecoats and slippers.

Soon we would go up to our bed, but the last thing we would hear would be that story. I would hear about the man whose picture was in the hall. I found out that we were celebrating his birthday. We sat in chairs in a circle around Miss Julie, and our heads were nodding with full bellies as the calming sound of her voice reading the ancient story settled us down. After the story, the group of excited girls would make it up to bed. I lay in my bed, once again trying to stay awake long enough to hear the soft prayer whispered over me in the night.

The orphanage did not deny us Santa, but we heard the reason for all the fun and parties and delicious treats. Santa was celebrating the birthday of Jesus.

One day, a Barbara Ann Scott doll was brought to the school for show and tell. She was known as Canada's Sweetheart, a two-time world figure skating champion.

She won the championship in 1948, but the doll continued to be a favorite Christmas gift for little girls into the end of the fifties.

We passed the doll around and were enthralled to see her miniature snowy costume. Every little girl longed for a doll of her own. We touched the furry edge of her costume and admired her skates.

When Santa came to visit on Christmas Day, he gave each of us that special doll. Squeals of delight filled the room as each girl opened a box with a doll in it. Mine was dressed in white. My favorite of all the dolls.

On that Christmas morning, we were still in our nighties and slippers. Breakfast was pancakes with syrup. None of us were trading food or giggling under the table. We ate every bite.

The night terrors became less frequent. I no longer woke up crying every night.

The memories of the orphanage provided me with a foundation; it did not prevent the darkness ahead, but as we long for the feel of the sun in the middle of a long dark winter, I would never forget the light of those years. Remembering the sun of those days in the long frigid winter of my life. In those days to come, I would long for a new spring and life to return to my frozen world. However, that Christmas, I was safe.

Chapter 4

FORBIDDEN FRUIT

"You must not do that; you will break your teeth."
Tossing chestnuts back and forth after school on a beautiful fall day was one of my favorite games, storing them in the pockets of my jacket, which were wonderfully big. They were often bulging with treasures. The girls were in competition with each other as we scrambled to gather the chestnuts that had fallen, laughing when we discovered one first and popped it in our pocket. At the end of the day, we would count them and see who had the most. The little nuggets of chestnuts were hard, but we tossed them up in the air, making our own fun.

Their smell was quite different to me. At seven years of age, I liked to smell everything I picked up, trying to catch an odor. They did not emit a smell, and I was going to take a bite, so Miss Julie warned me quickly. She came and entered the fun on those fall afternoons after school. We were glad when she played with us. She had wonderful ideas.

"Maybe we will try roasting them," she said. "You will be able to smell them when they are roasted. Once they are cooked, then the hard shell can be removed, and you can find out if you like them. Gather some up, and let's see if the cook will roast them for you."

After school, we gathered more chestnuts. Miss Julie and a group of girls took the stash we had gathered to the kitchen.

The cook helped us to wash them, and we placed them on a cooking tray and slipped them in the oven. Prior to putting them in the oven, she cut a slit into each chestnut.

"If we do not do that, they will explode in the oven," she explained, as she cut the slit in the chestnuts. We were all standing around her, watching everything, fascinated at her efficient moves as she made quick cuts in the chestnuts.

Several girls peered into the window of the oven door. As we waited, others wandered around the room, curious about everything in that massive kitchen.

We did not have to wait long and were allowed with the cook's help to watch the process and to try them. A light was put on in the oven, and we watched them expand as they cooked. When they cooled enough to taste them, we were not in love with the taste. However, the fun part was cooking them and exploring the kitchen.

Entering the kitchen and watching the cook preparing the nuts for us was my first experience of taking part in cooking food. The kitchen was a wonderful place for me, full of enticing smells. The cook was a plump lady and reminded me of all the cooks I had seen in my picture books. She had a full flowing dress with an apron and wore a little cap over her hair. I looked at her with delight. She did not seem real, even though I knew she was. She appeared perfect, with her flowing dress and apron.

When she bent down to talk to me, she smelled like the delicious food she was cooking. When I entered the kitchen, I was entering the heart of the orphanage, a comforting womb,

Two young women were cutting up vegetables on the counter. Everyone was cheerful and busy. They welcomed a bunch of curious girls pummeling them with questions.

We had a lot of questions as we watched for a few minutes as they deftly cut up carrots and celery. They told us it was to add to the large pot simmering on top of the stove.

The smells of the kitchen created its own harmony of delight.

"If you gather more chestnuts for me, we can add them to the stuffing in the turkey."

The cook was delighted with the ones we had gathered. We proudly set about finding more for her.

Although I enjoyed the fun of the chestnuts, my favorite taste was the sweet apples.

Apple trees grew close to the orphanage along the perimeter of the property on the other side of a fence. They were full of apples ready to fall and easy to pick. Their scent filled the air. We girls had been warned not to climb the apple trees. As we approached the orphanage after school, that scent grew strong, and our stomachs would growl in anticipation. We were ready for a snack when we arrived home from school.

"Now girls, you must not climb the apple trees," said the captain.

A warning from the captain should be taken seriously. She was an important person. She was the boss of everyone and had her own office near the front door of the estate; we did not see her often, other than at mealtimes. A trip to the captain's office meant we were in trouble. Her word must be obeyed.

"These apples do not belong to us. The only apples you can gather are the ones that fall on our side of the fence. You must not climb the trees for two reasons. You may get hurt, and those apples belong to our neighbors."

She stood at the front of the dining room and delivered her stern warning. We were sitting at our tables, and we all sat in silence.

I was a little afraid of her. She wore a uniform and reminded me of a police officer.

Coming home from school with the scent of the apples on the air, we would run over to the fence and quickly pick up whatever apples we could find on our side.

It was a mad dash to see who could get to them first. Sometimes, there weren't any, and we stood and looked longingly up at the trees. The apples we could not get at lay on the grass in their ripeness. We were noisy, giggling, and calling out to each other. We had a short time after school to try and grab some and then we had to hurry into the orphanage.

There was often someone looking out the windows of the building next door, peering down at us; we felt they were not pleased with the noise we were making. Sometimes, a dog came out and barked at us and growled menacingly This only added to our nervousness and excitement. We were glad we were separated by the fence. A large black squirrel glared at us from the apple tree. It knew we were competing for the apples. Animals had personalities and feelings. I would look at them and try to read them. They were not welcoming us.

One day, a power outage freed a group of us girls early from school. The day was a mixture of sun and dark clouds that were approaching on the horizon. It was warm for fall, with the remnants of summer still lingering with the stillness of an approaching storm, heavy and humid.

There was pressure in the air that was building before some of those clouds would burst, and in the distance, there was the periodic sound of thunder.

"Let's hurry to the apple trees," I called out to the other girls. The smell of the apples and the unexpected free time was too much temptation. The other girls gave me an enthusiastic response.

"Yes! Yes!"

We were excited and even more so because there was a risk. Those trees had been such a temptation. We had stood at the fence many times and longed to climb them.

We had a bit of time, so we hurried to the trees. Apples were heavy on the branches, full and ripe, and I did not want the squirrels to get them while they lay rotting on the ground. They would rot, and we would not be able to eat them, as the softer they got, they came alive with worms.

As we got closer to the orphanage, the smell of the apples intensified. On that muggy day, they were cooking on the trees. We hurried, as we knew we did not have much time. I was hoping to fill my pockets with them.

What could be the harm? Why should the squirrels and worms have those apples?

"Quickly," I urged my fellow conspirators. We ran over to the trees.

I took my jacket off and threw it on the ground. We girls were alone. Another girl followed my lead, and two girls stood apart on the grass below the tree, holding on to the jacket and spreading it between them to create a canopy for me to toss apples on. Another girl stood watching in case an adult discovered us. Two of us climbed onto the fence. I was thankful the dog was not around.

I clambered up the fence, and reaching the top, I stretched to grab an apple from a branch. I was focused on a particularly large apple, and the world around me faded in that attempt, oblivious to any danger.

Another girl stood lower on the fence and had her hand around my ankle, trying to keep me steady as in my stretching, I released one foot from the fence. The red apple overcame my nervousness. It loomed before me in a giant proportion. It was the biggest apple I had seen. Red and full of goodness.

The clouds drew closer, darkening the sky. The sound of thunder grew louder, and a flash of lightning startled the girls.

The girls on the ground scattered quickly, and my fellow climber released her grip and made her way down. I was left hanging. I had grasped my hand around that apple and had started to pull with all my strength.

"June!"

The sound of running feet and the shout reached my ears at the top of the fence.

Simultaneously, a lightning bolt flashed across the sky, and I jerked back instinctively from the branch and lost my balance. Down I tumbled, hitting the ground with a thump. I kept my grip around the apple.

Pain filled my body, and now, flat on my back, I looked up, and one of the ladies from the orphanage was bending over me with a mixture of concern and anger. This was not Miss Julie but another of the young women who cared for us. She reached her hand down to me. I took her hand and was helped up. I quickly picked up my jacket and slipped the apple into the pocket.

We walked back to the orphanage and headed for the captain's office. This was serious business. I was in trouble. The captain was waiting for us. News had gotten to her quickly. She rose from her desk and stood before me sternly.

"June, you have disobeyed me," she said.

She had a ruler in her hand, and I missed most of her words because my eyes were focused on that ruler. It was a flexible steel ruler, and it looked wicked. The edge of the ruler was sharp. The lecture was getting lost.

"Hold your hand out," she instructed.

I got three whacks. My other hand gripped the apple in my pocket throughout the whacks.

I tried not to cry but ended up in tears, and then I started to shake. Immediately, a look of concern crossed the captain's face, and she drew me close in a hug.

"I'm sorry," I sobbed.

We pulled away from each other, and I was free to go. I ran up the long winding stairs into the washroom, where I washed my face and dried my eyes. I took a few deep breaths to stop the shaking. Facing the girls with weepy eyes and a splotchy complexion felt like failure.

Stiffening my shoulders, I went downstairs into the great room, where the girls were waiting for me. Holding my head up, I joined them, my hand wrapped around that apple.

"What happened?" they whispered excitedly.

I opened my hand and showed them the apple; I had paid a heavy price for that apple. I wanted them to focus on the prize, not the consequences.

"Oh, I just got a few smacks."

Miss Julie came over, placed her arm around me, and broke up the huddle of girls. She was not fooled by my bravado.

"Come," she said quietly. We walked downstairs to the playroom and went over to my toy box, and I opened it up. The key that locked it had disappeared a long time ago. Miss Julie handed me a new book. I climbed into the box.

"Just until supper," she said.

I nodded my head back at her mutely, worried I would start to cry again.

The first bite of the apple was honey on my tongue.

Chapter 5

CANDIES AND LOVE

What would it be like to be loved like that?
I was lost in my imagination. Standing in front of a large picture of Jesus with a child on his lap and children around him, I asked myself the question. This man became the dad of my heart. Miss Julie was my mom, and he was my dad. The girls were my sisters. My brother was just away for a while, but he would come back to me one day. I made up my own dreams.

I would stare at the picture and get lost in it, imagining jumping into the scene and joining the children laughing around him and feeling his arms around me, I adopted him as my imaginary dad. My own father had died when I was less than one year old.

Other girls often joined me, and we stood together, likely wondering the same thing. In a way, we were in the same boat together, separated from our families. We had a common bond and shared our joys and sorrows. In the orphanage, there were common joys.

All of us had a favorite day each week. On that day, we bounced out of bed with anticipation.

It was Friday.

In the morning, we hurried and got dressed and ran down the winding stairs for breakfast. Friday was full of treats. Two treats happened after breakfast.

One was our weekly allowance, and the other was our spoonful of cod liver oil malt. We lined up after breakfast to receive our money and held our hands out to receive pennies.

"Don't spend it all at once."

Miss Julie winked at us when she said that. It was her joke, as we always spent it all at once at a little candy store near the school.

We licked our spoons of the sweet tasting syrup and took our two pennies. They went into our sequined little purses with our names embroidered on them. They each had a zipper, and we carefully put our pennies in it and closed the zipper.

We guarded them carefully, as our trip to the store had to wait until the end of the school day.

With our sequined purses clutched in our eager hands, we flocked to the store to purchase our penny bags of candy. A bunch of awestruck girls stood in front of what appeared like mountains of candies on display.

The store owner stood behind that counter and beamed at us every Friday.

We imagined having all those candies. We took a long time choosing our treats. The man behind the counter was always welcoming and friendly to a troop of girls filling his small store every Friday after school.

Most of the girls would gulp their candy down. I would make mine last longer for trading.

The bubble gum lasted until it couldn't be chewed. I would meticulously wrap the chewed gum in a wrapper to make it last until it was like chewing rubber, even enjoying the rubber taste. My goal was to make it last until I received my next allowance.

After bringing home my purchase, I would go down to my toy box and hide some of the candies in the little jewelry box, removing the play jewelry and storing my hoard. Most of the girls had lost their keys, so we had an honor system.

We did not forage in each other's boxes.

If I wanted to barter for a special favor, I would use those treats as my money and trade with the other girls. At school, I sometimes got a treat for singing. I did quite well.

Several girls did not mind giving up a book for a couple of candies.

One winter, we were all quarantined for mumps. We lay in our beds, bored. Not sick enough to be inactive but not too sick to create our own fun. Restless and penned up, we found ways to amuse ourselves. We pretended we were sleepwalking.

It was my turn to pretend, and I got out of bed and closed my eyes. I raised my arms up before me straight and I ran, giggling. It was our version of blind man's bluff.

We wrapped a towel around our eyes. I was going to be a running sleepwalker. In the middle of a bunch of bored little girls. I was excited and got carried away with all the attention on me, and my physical awkwardness had its way.

Wham. I ran right into the end of a bed. I bumped into it heavily, and my front teeth went through my lower lip. I went flying.

Chaos ensued; some of the girls went screaming for Miss Julie, and I lay on the floor, writhing with pain. I was rushed to the hospital and had to be stitched. That day, I did not try to hide my cries.

I was prone to accidents. The more excited I got, the more I dropped things and bumped into walls, as I was a dreamer, walking around in my own world, creating worlds of my imagination, centered on making imaginary stories in my head. I often created an alternative reality about the family I had lost. Longing for a family, I formed an attachment to Miss Julie and was having difficulty sharing her with the other girls. In my mind, she had become my mummy, and I took to games like limping, pretending I had an injury to gain her attention.

About this time, it was discovered I was shortsighted, which contributed to my awkwardness, so soon I was sporting glasses, which I had the habit of removing and losing.

Engrossed in a book, I would walk away and leave my glasses behind; I ended up spending a lot of time looking for my glasses.

I learned to amuse myself by taking on some of the roles of the people in my books. I loved to make up stories before I fell asleep at night,

I pretended I owned a horse and visualized riding down the middle of the street on my horse: my own version of Lady Godiva.

While we were quarantined for mumps, we were given paper money, and a store was set up in the playroom in the basement. On a table were paper bags, and crayons and a little coloring book were in each bag. The bags were decorated with a funny sticker and contained a small puzzle.

We were given paper money, amounting to two cents. The money was for us to choose from bowls of candies and gum and suckers.

The friendly cook from the kitchen was behind a table. She still wore her hat and her smile and her flowing dress and apron. In her hand, she held a scoop, and in front of her were two bins of ice cream and a stack of cones, ready to fill with ice cream.

The time of quarantine ended, and other than my episode with the sleepwalking, it was not difficult for any of us and went by quickly.

There were also times of special outings. In the fall, we went to the Canadian National Expo, or CNE. We stayed together at the huge fair by holding onto a rope. It was a big challenge to keep us from straggling away, especially on the midway.

Miss Julie accompanied me on the scarier rides, and she was excited too. We both screamed and laughed. I particularly liked the roller coaster but would not go on it alone.

The tilt-a-whirl was another favorite but unfortunately made me sick. We would go from ride to ride, and Miss Julie and the other staff had quite a job to keep us in some form of discipline.

We were all introduced to candy floss and giggled so much at the mess we made of the sticky fluff. Six and seven-year-old girls with candy floss was funny. The more sugar we had in our small bodies, the louder we were.

We started playing with the sticky candy, taking off chunks and discovering we could stick it to each other. Miss Julie stopped that game quickly, but I am certain all our dresses became a sticky mess, as did our hair.

Filled with the fun of it all, whatever sadness we carried was forgotten, for a little while.

The system of two to three long ropes with one of the young women at each end and the girls hanging on to the rope worked. We threaded in and around the crowds.

None of us straggled away. There were thirty young girls, so that was quite remarkable. I do not recall anyone getting lost.

That night, when we arrived back at the orphanage, we stripped off our sticky dresses and had baths. It was difficult to fall asleep with all that sugar inside.

I created my Lady Godiva story in my head as I fell asleep. I may have embellished it, imagining I was riding my horse in the middle of the CNE.

The orphanage was starting to heal my wounded heart. Days and weeks went by, and grief started to abate. I knew the orphanage was a different family, but I thought it might be enough.

Although the family at the orphanage seemed okay for me, the days were ending, and the search for a new family started. The oasis I had been living on was simply that. It was a temporary oasis. The bird would soon leave the nest.

Chapter 6
THE FARM

"I have to pee!" I said, hopping up and down.

"Quickly," Miss Julie said, grabbing my hand.

Miss Julie knew that accidents had happened when I was excited, and she rushed me out of the line. We did not want a repeat of the incident that happened before.

The last one took place when I was sitting with the girls in the great room, watching *The Little Rascals*. I was laughing so hard, and then, whoops. Miss Julie and I jumped out of our seats and hurried out of the darkened room.

At five years of age that day, I was old enough to be embarrassed and to have a red face. Miss Julie had been kind. We cleaned up in the washroom, and I quickly changed my clothes. We slipped back into the great room and joined the girls watching the movie. We quietly found a new seat at the back.

However, two years later, when I was seven years old, we did not waste time hurrying to the washroom. There was a lineup of girls in the great room, and Miss Julie and I were standing in line. We were waiting to be introduced to prospective foster parents. Someone had decided I could be fostered. Miss Julie tried to convince me that I should be part of a family. My problem with that was I would be torn away from her. I trusted her and was willing to try. Starting to accept the loss of my family, I was being guided to look for a substitute. This lineup was the first step in that process. I was going to be inspected.

Dressed in my Sunday best and waiting in line, I was nervous.

This was a Miss Mini Orphan contest. First prize would be a mom and dad. The inspection lineups created a mixture of anxiety and hope. Waking up early that morning, the preparation had taken some time.

The night before, Miss Julie had told me about the couple I was going to meet. I had a tough time getting to sleep, tossing and turning in my bed. Miss Julie had made everything sound wonderful, and I was excited.

"Mr. and Mrs. Thomas live on a farm. They have a boy and a girl close to your age. They also have a dog and a cat."

She told me it was a dairy farm; they had cows.

"It would be good for you to be part of a family."

The idea of a farm and animals intrigued me. However, I woke up during the night, and Miss Julie had held me and sang one of her songs.

With fears starting to fade in the morning light, I was caught up in the preparations and excitement. My best dress was brought out, and the orphanage was busy with little girls being fussed over. I was getting a chance to dress up, which was one of my favorite things.

Miss Julie had shampooed my hair that morning. At the age of seven, I hated my hair. It was super fine and curly and often full of tangles. Untangling it was painful.

"Ouch," I'd cry.

"Sit still," they'd say.

A special dress had been laid out on my bed. It was pink with frills and puffed sleeves. This delighted me, and I pulled it over my head and started to swirl around, as the skirt was full.

A pink bow that matched the dress was pinned to my unruly hair to try and keep it tidy. I was having a tough time staying still as this preparation went on, and my excitement was rising.

A pair of black patent leather shoes with a bow on the front had been placed on my feet.

I started twirling around and dancing with those shoes on. Miss Julie and I started clapping and singing the Billy Bland song as we did this: "Let the little girl dance, let the little girl dance."

We forgot for the moment what we were doing. Miss Julie was young enough to enjoy being silly with me in the middle of all this serious business. We both broke out in laughter. I was caught up in the whole idea of being a real princess in my dancing shoes and my pretty dress.

All this happened in the preparation for the inspection lineup. We finished our preparations, and the girls gathered in the great room, waiting to be inspected.

We had been standing at the end of the line when I told Miss Julie I needed to pee. After a quick trip to the washroom, my hair was fluffed up, and we joined the lineup again. Miss Julie and I took our place at the back. All the girls were dressed up in their best dresses, and we were giggling and nervous, so there was a lot of chattering in the room as we waited. Only one girl would be chosen.

What if I'm not cute enough? I worried. Being cute was important.

I was a bundle of mixed emotions. I was glad Miss Julie stood beside me.

I watched, standing still for a moment, as a lady made her way down the line towards us. Snow White with her bright red lipstick and shiny hair walked down the line, stooping to speak to each child.

A tall man with thick, dark wavy hair walked along with her; to me, he looked like the handsome prince.

Where were the seven dwarfs? I could be one.

They continued to move closer, and my excitement grew.

Could this be real? Could this really happen?

I was filled with hopes and dreams, and the pressure was building. I jiggled around impatiently, waiting for them to get closer.

"Shush," Miss Julie whispered. "Stay still."

I started to move out of the line and go towards them, but she held me back with her hand, which was not easy, as I was squirming around in those patent leather shoes and jumping up and down with excitement.

Here she was, bending down before me. As she leaned down to me, I could smell her: flowers and soap.

It was love at first sight.

"You are pretty," she said softly.

The compliment filled me with pleasure, and I could feel my face flush. Suddenly, I was filled with shyness. I stopped my jiggling, quieted down, and stood still.

Looking up at the man standing next to her, the lady raised her eyebrows in a silent question. The man nodded his head. She turned to Miss Julie.

"She will do."

Nothing further was said to me.

The line dispersed. We had been told that we would wait for the news of who had been chosen, but I had seen the nod.

When I went to bed that night, my dreams were filled with anticipation. The next morning, Miss Julie told me I had been invited to stay with that couple for a week at their farm.

She packed a bag for me, and they picked me up in their car. I sat in the back seat, and the lady turned around to chat on the journey. I was in awe of them. The car was full of the woman's same flowery scent.

Mrs. Thomas told me about their farm, and I learned they had a dairy farm and grew fields of corn and wheat.

On the way to the farm, the city disappeared. We passed open fields. The drive felt long to me, and finally, we left the main road and turned into their long driveway, which was bordered by trees. Black-and-white cows were grazing in the fields.

Everything was open and bright. The sky was a brilliant blue, and the clouds were white drifts with a hint of darkness on the edges.

The midday sun made it hot in the car. Mrs. Thomas had opened my window slightly. The air coming in was a welcome freshness to the heat and was different than the city air. There were few cars on the road we had left. I could see a tractor in the distance, and I smelled freshly mowed grass and the scent of animals. In the background of the quiet day, I heard the calls of geese.

I sat in the back seat, hushed and still. This was my first introduction to the country, and I was caught up in the beauty that was enfolding before me.

Some distant memory deep in my soul had been stirred up, and I felt peace. My mother and my father and Freddie and I had lived in the north in Canada when I was a baby.

The memories of those early days remained in the recesses of my mind, as something familiar was rising in me. It was not an unpleasant memory. Did my brother and I play together in the north, in those early days when my father was alive?

These were new sensations, and I silently enjoyed the view and the smells of the country. In my experience, buildings hid the view of the sky, but I could see it that day.

Someone had pulled aside the dark curtains in the window of the world and let me see the daylight. The world expanded into a vast landscape, full of beauty and light.

We drove up the tree-lined driveway; there was a farmhouse at the end of it and in the background, I could see a couple of other buildings. One of them was an old red barn. The scene whispered peace.

There were three buildings. One held the cows, and another held the hay. The third was the farmhouse, and that house was surrounded with gardens and wildflowers moving in the light breeze. Across the front of the house was a wide porch that wound around the exterior of the front, filled with welcoming chairs of every variety, including rocking chairs.

Would this be my new home? I wondered. *Would I finally have a family?*

The car slowed down, and a black dog ran out to greet us, running in circles and barking. There were two children playing outside; they turned to us and started running with the dog towards the car. The older child was a boy, and the girl was closer to my age. They were happy to see us. Their faces were beaming as they ran up to us. They had tanned faces and tawny-colored hair bleached from the sun.

The car stopped. As I opened the door and stepped out of the car, Mrs. Thomas introduced me to the kids. The girl's name was Sandra, and her brother's name was Ron.

While Mrs. Thomas went into the kitchen to prepare lunch, Sandra took my hand and showed me to our bedroom on the second level. The room had two beds in it. I was glad to know I would be sharing a room with her.

There was a large cat sitting on one of the beds, and Sandra shooed it off.

Nervously, I stood still when I saw the cat, as she was not happy at being disturbed, and she looked like a mini monster to me.

What was that noise she made? I wondered.

The noise the cat made was familiar and triggered in me the memory of another cat many years ago. She bared her teeth when she made it. I stumbled as I stepped back quickly out of her way. She jumped off the bed at the same time making that noise. Sandra laughed at my fear. The cat slowly moved out of the room and the way she stalked away gave me the feeling that she was annoyed at being disturbed. I found out later she was full of babies.

The window was wide open. The breeze coming in was ruffling the sheer curtains in the room. Both beds had quilted covers. The borders were edged in pastel flowers of pink and blue, and white lambs were in the center of quilted squares.

The quilted covers and fluffy pillows created a feeling of comfort. Strewn around the room on the beds and on the shelf were stuffed animals and dolls. There was a pair of Raggedy Ann dolls to which I was drawn. Sandra could see my eyes go to them sitting on her bed.

"Pick them up," she said to me shyly.

I went over to them and picked them up, one at a time. I was fascinated with them.

"You can have one on your bed while you are here," she said.

I was delighted.

Mrs. Thomas called up, "Lunch is ready!"

We went down to the large kitchen, which had a mammoth table and filled half of the room. Several men sitting around it.

They looked strong and had tanned faces with windblown hair. Many workers were needed for that large farm. There were four men, with Mr. Thomas making the fifth. They talked and laughed, and their energy and strength enlivened the kitchen.

Two of the men were standing and helping themselves to the food. Ron, the young boy, was with them. He looked happy, and I could see he loved being with his dad and the workers. The table was loaded with food, and the smell made my mouth water. Something was cooking away on the stove and emitting steam. The room was fragrant with fresh bread that had come out of the oven.

The kitchen held a large refrigerator and freezer.

The cupboards were stained in a beautiful light wood and lined the walls of half the room, with long counters and a large island in the center, topped with a wooden cutting board. On that island were two fresh loaves of bread and a carving knife alongside. The men were helping themselves to the bread. A bowl of creamy butter accompanied the loaves.

The large table was set for lunch and covered with an oilcloth. A vase held a variety of flowers, which I found out later grew wild on the farm.

The aromas, the warmth, the laughter, and the conversation mingled, creating an aura of sounds and smells, including the smells of animals.

Usually, those smells were well camouflaged by the cooking, but sometimes, they drifted through the open windows in strong waves. One of those waves hit me, and I was puzzled.

This was a new smell for me. Sandra laughed at the expression on my face when I looked at her with surprise. She knew right away what I was smelling.

"That is a healthy smell," she said.

An old sofa was placed against a wall, along with a rocking chair. An elderly woman was sitting on the chair, knitting. I walked over and said hi to her, curious to see what she was knitting.

She looked at me; she was beautiful, with long grey hair swept up. She looked up at me with warm, welcoming eyes.

She was knitting something that was multicolored. It fell over her knee and was close to the floor. I was struck by the beauty of it, and I looked at it with fascination and curiosity. Her hands worked swiftly and skillfully. She did not stop her knitting as she looked at me, smiled warmly, and returned my greeting.

I went back to the table and joined Sandra. She handed me a plate; I had my eyes on the fragrant bread and went over to the center island to help myself. Everything was made on the farm, even the butter that was slathered generously on the bread.

Watching the butter churning was another new experience. I wanted to put my finger into the creamy goodness. One day, we had fresh corn with that butter melting on it.

The farm had beehives, and I was treated to some of that honey.

Well-worn habits of assigned chores and duties filled the days. Sandra and I were given simple tasks and expected to help with the dishes and clean up. We set the tables, and because of the novelty of it all, it did not feel like work.

We had fun helping to hang laundry to dry on the long lines stretched between two poles. We held a basket of clothespins and handed them to Mrs. Thomas.

We were more hindrance than help, though, because our playfulness took over, and we ran through the sheets, playing peekaboo. I loved seeing the clothes blowing in the lovely summer breezes. Later, Sandra and I would help fold some of the clothes, and I kept holding them to my nose and sniffing them, as they smelled of the sun and fresh air.

Escorting the cows back to the barn from their grazing in the evenings' soft twilight became my favorite event. The end of a sweltering summer day, as the sun started to set, was a scene of beauty.

We walked alongside the black-and-white cows and the air became alive with flies and mosquitoes. They buzzed around the cows and around me. The cows nonchalantly swished their tales at them as we walked along. The bugs liked my fair skin. Unlike the cows, I was maddened by them, waving my arms around me.

I got quite a few bites. Bug spray was unheard of, and no one other than me seemed to be bothered by them.

The blazing sun disappeared into the horizon as the day ended. We became quiet as we walked along beside the cows. This was a stunning part of the day, and there was a peace that descended on all of us. A stillness, as we could not resist the effect of the perfect sunset. The setting rays transformed our walk.

The cows were a curiosity, but I was nervous around them. I stayed close to Sandra, who was not nervous at all, and her calmness reassured me. The black dog trotted quietly along with us on those walks.

I can still hear the music of the birds in my head and the scene in my mind, as we walked along with the cows. The singing birds created their own symphony of music that was magnified in the stillness of the sweltering day. Sandra and the dog walked beside the cows. Mr. Thomas and Ron led the way up front. The black-and-white cows strolled leisurely along in between us. For a few moments, time stopped.

When we entered the red barn, the cows were back home. This was time for fun.

We'd jump from the barn's hayloft into the soft mounds of hay, squealing from the thrill. Getting up and shaking off the hay prickling my skin and doing it repeatedly. The children in the family delighted in my excitement. They were urging me on, and the black dog ran around us in circles, barking and entering in the fun.

The cat continued to avoid me when I tried to make friends with her. She sat and watched us unblinkingly, staring at us: the only creature that was not happy with all the fuss and noise. I felt her disapproval, like a stern parent looking at our silliness. Tolerating it, but not amused.

When we got back in the evening, there were snacks waiting us. Often a fresh muffin and chocolate milk, which we would wolf down.

Rainy days, well, we dressed for them. Sandra lent me her rain rubbers and a jacket. Only thunder and lightning sent us indoors.

Each night, I slept in a soft bed with a full tummy and the exhaustion of an active day. I felt part of the family, and for that time, everything was perfect.

After the week was up, I had to return to the orphanage.

When Sandra said goodbye, she handed me the Raggedy Ann doll and told me to keep it.

"Until we see each other again," Sandra said shyly.

Mrs. Thomas handed me a parcel; inside was a replica of the lovely blanket the elderly woman was making. I looked up, and she was standing inside the screened door, waving at me.

Back at the orphanage, everything had turned a dull grey.

Chapter 7

BEING A GIRL

One morning, Miss Julie nudged me gently on the shoulder and took my hand. We went upstairs and sat in the front of the bay window at the end of the hall.

The sun lit up the room. There was a small sofa under the window and an easy chair, intended for the intimacy of soft conversations.

We sat down under the window; the sunlight lit up Miss Julie's hair, which she wore down that day. Her eyes were filled with sadness, and I could see tears forming.

My heart sank.

The noise outside and around us left. Tears started flowing down Miss Julie's face.

I was drowning in them and stopped breathing. In those tears, my dreams and hopes faded and retreated and fell with them.

I had been so sure I was finally going to be part of a family.

The sun slipped behind a cloud, and the room grew darker.

"I am sorry," Miss Julie managed to say. "They wanted a boy."

So, there we sat, both of us weeping in that silent place.

Chapter 8

THE BIRD LEAVES THE NEST

Sitting once again in front of the same bow window a few weeks later, Miss Julie and I met once more. We were facing each other in the sunlit room. This time, she looked pleased. I was leaving the orphanage.

She sat across from me on the sofa, and in her arms, she had a soft, floppy-eared stuffed animal. She handed it to me.

"I want you to have this," she said.

"Will I be able to take my toy box?"

"Of course. You are ready. You are a big girl now and need to be part of a family that will love you."

I did not feel like a big girl. I recently had my eighth birthday, and in that moment, I felt small again. I would be leaving the place I had grown to love. Once again, the ground was shaking under my feet. I felt betrayed and confused. She was trying to convince me there was nothing I had done wrong. I was not persuaded. Feeling unwanted, I was beginning to believe there was something wrong with me. On the heels of the rejection of the people at the farm, I did not know what to believe.

"This is for your own good," felt like the words of punishment.

I was not sure it was for my own good at all.

Miss Julie was enthusiastic, but I sensed something was off. Uneasiness settled into my heart. It was too much enthusiasm. I had heard it all before prior to going to the farm for the week.

She leaned forward and said earnestly, "You will have your own room."

She knew how much I longed for privacy in the middle of an orphanage, sharing my room with several girls.

"You will be the only child, and the people you will be living with have been waiting a long time for a girl."

Being a girl was now good?

It was very confusing.

"Are you coming with me?" I asked.

Miss Julie explained that she could not come. I did not know if I would see her again. I hugged myself and tried to stop shaking.

We left the room, and Miss Julie helped me pack my things. We went downstairs together. I remembered that first day when I had walked up those beautiful wide stairs, a five-year-old girl full of grief at the loss of her family. Now I was walking down those stairs and out that front door. Leaving the orphanage was a different kind of grief. I was leaving Miss Julie.

My toy box was sitting in the front hall, and my clothes were packed. I held tight to the floppy-eared stuffed animal.

I am a big girl now, I told myself.

A few hours later, a small woman who reminded me of Peter Pan picked me up at the orphanage. Miss Julie told me this lady was my social worker and would take me to my new home.

She had a pixie hairstyle, wispy bangs, and big brown eyes with glasses that made her eyes look bigger and her button nose smaller, with a thin mouth. She was not tall, as I came up to her shoulders.

As promised, my toy box was placed in her car.

"Hi, June," she said. "I am Miss Sweet."

She proffered her hand to me, and I shook it. She was friendly and calm, managing my toy box and my suitcase with ease.

Transferring young, confused, teary-eyed children from place to place didn't seem to ruffle her, and her detachment worked in a strange way because to her, what was happening was insignificant. No big deal.

The person who was anxious and fussing was Miss Julie herself. As we went downstairs to collect my things, she tried to hide it, but I could see she was upset.

There was no inspection line that had introduced me to the people I was about to meet.

Miss Julie and I said our final tear-filled goodbye. We hugged each other, and I got into the car with Miss Sweet. I was filled with sadness, anxiety, and fear. I remember looking at that beautiful estate and the figure of Miss Julie standing and waving goodbye to me as we drove away. Her shadow in the distance got smaller, and my heart was once again filled with grief.

I did not feel like a big girl.

I was leaving the Nest.

Chapter 9
A NEW HOME

The figure of Miss Julie at the front door, waving goodbye, and the beautiful estate in the background is an image that remains with me. Parts of Miss Julie have faded from my memory, but I remember her heart, the soul of a woman who embraced a small child and let me play with her hair and danced with me and twirled me around and visited me in the middle of my night terrors. She unwittingly created a foundation that although shaken terribly by the darkness that lay ahead for me, she would still come for me in the dark watches of the nights of terror I would face. In a world where religion carried an evil face, she instead offered me a different kind of face, the face of love drawn from the God she worshiped and formed into the image of the man in the picture of the orphanage. I would run from that religion, but that image remained. The shadow of Miss Julie fading did not remove that image.

It was the last time I saw Miss Julie.

Sitting in the car that was driving me away from Miss Julie was Miss Sweet. I wondered who this woman was. Miss Julie said she was my social worker, but this was the first time I recall meeting a social worker. I did not know what a social worker was.

Can I trust her? I wondered.

I did not know this lady. Suddenly, my life was altered abruptly, and I sensed this woman was part of that decision to alter it. She exuded self-assurance.

Her efficient and self-assured manner was intimidating to my eight-year-old self. I felt smaller in her presence.

Someone had decided that I should leave the orphanage and be part of a foster family, and I had no voice in the matter. I suspected neither did Miss Julie. Did she know anything?

I prayed I would not be further hurt. I turned my face forward as Miss Sweet and I headed to what lay ahead.

It was getting close to lunch. Miss Sweet pulled into the parking lot of a restaurant. That day, I would be introduced to what would become a ritual.

After a grilled cheese sandwich and fries, we finished with a butterscotch sundae.

The ice cream with the caramel syrup and whipped cream had a calming effect on me when I put that creamy goodness in my mouth.

I would find out that indeed a spoonful of ice cream did help the medicine go down. Especially if it was covered with syrup and whipped cream with a red cherry on top.

I listened to Miss Sweet as she began to describe the couple we were going to meet. I sat there uneasily, wanting to believe her. However, the experience with the people at the farm had shaken me. I had been sure they wanted me, but they did not. My heart was guarded but could not deny the small stirring of anticipation as she described where I was being taken. Miss Sweet spoke softly and convincingly, reducing my fear, but I was wary. I knew that adults did not always tell the truth.

I nodded my head and wanted to believe. Her calm manner and the sundae did their work to ease my fears.

I clutched the floppy-eared stuffed animal tighter to me and listened.

Soon we were on our way to my new home, which was in the east end of Toronto. It was a detached two-story home on a pleasant tree-lined street.

We walked to the front door and did not have to knock, as the door immediately opened, and we were welcomed inside by a woman.

Stepping inside, I was instantly captivated with the television. The orphanage did not have a television. Distracted, I ran over to it.

"June, this is Mr. and Mrs. James," said Miss Sweet.

I turned around and quickly stepped closer to the woman, who stood waiting. I was given a hug.

It was an uncomfortable hug, as it was tight and close, which I tolerated for a few seconds but squirmed away from. Being hugged like that was claustrophobic. It felt desperate.

Freeing myself and stepping back, I looked at the woman who was standing before me. When she hugged me, I caught a trace of cigarette smoke, mingled with a pleasant light perfume. That scent triggered a memory of another woman a long time ago.

The smiling lady who stood before me had short auburn hair, immaculately styled. She wore makeup. None of the young women at the orphanage donned makeup. She had on a pair of pearl earrings and a matching pearl necklace. The dress she wore was a midnight blue, which was my favorite color. I was impressed with the way Mrs. James looked.

The couple was older than the people at the farm. When Mrs. James spoke, she had an enjoyable way of speaking, an accent which I later found out was British.

"Welcome, June," she said. "We hope you will be happy here."

I was not sure what to do. I had the impulse to make a little curtsy. The lady standing before me was pleasant. She had a welcoming smile, but I sensed regality. There was no casualness in her dress or manner.

Now I was introduced to her husband. He was sitting quietly in the background in the corner of the room. He was a small balding man with glasses.

He was also dressed formally with a sweater and a shirt and tie.

"Hello, June. Welcome."

He was soft-spoken and had an accent, but it was slightly different than his wife. He had a warm twinkle in his eyes.

A pipe was in his hand, but he was not smoking it. He put down the newspaper he was reading, got up from his chair, and greeted me with a quick hug. Unlike his wife, it was not close. I liked that hug better. I liked the smell of pipe smoke.

Later, I would watch him go through the ritual in the lighting and the smoking of the pipe. I would find myself watching with curiosity. The sheer pleasure he registered at his first puff made me want to experience it.

"Could I try it too?" I asked one day.

"Sure," he said. His eyes sparkled with delight.

He stood back and let me try it, watching me for my reaction, and I broke into a coughing fit as a bit of the strong tobacco smoke hit my throat. I handed the pipe back to him quickly, and that was the end of that. He had a good chuckle about it.

On the day of my arrival, Miss Sweet went out to the car and brought my toy box in. I was relieved to see it and ran over, delighted to see there were new surprises in the box.

Miss Julie had put some high-heeled shoes and a pretty scarf and a floppy hat for dress-up inside. There were also new books.

I peered into the box in the front hall while Miss Sweet and Mrs. James exchanged a few words; I was distracted at my new gifts. I promptly wrapped the scarf around my neck and plunked the hat on my head. I quickly put the heels on and started clucking around the room in excitement in my own world, oblivious of anything else that was happening.

I began tottering and wobbling on the shoes, and Mrs. James shouted out and reached towards me to stop me from falling over.

"No! No!" she shouted out, grabbing me. Her shout startled me.

I started to fall. I was close to a table with a vase of flowers on it. I fell and knocked over the table, and everything crashed to the floor, along with the flowers, which were thankfully artificial.

The change in Mrs. James's manner was startling, as her face became red, and her pleasant manner disappeared. My momentary security crumbled, and fear rose. She bent over and picked everything up as I stood back, mortified. Fortunately, the vase was not broken, but the change in the room was electric.

"You only wear shoes in the basement or outside."

Looking for Miss Sweet, I saw that she was at the front door, preparing to leave. I walked over to her, reaching out.

She gave me a quick hug, said goodbye, opened the door, and was gone. Her quick exit left me standing, looking at the closed door. Abandoned, as the door closed behind her.

After Miss Sweet left, Mrs. James took me upstairs and showed me my bedroom.

Perhaps this will be okay, I thought. Wearing shoes in the house was the big deal and my mistake. We were moving on.

Mr. James carried my toy box up to my room.

There were two bedrooms and a washroom on the upper level. When we walked into my bedroom, I could see how much effort had been made to make the room attractive to me. I would have a room all to myself. I could not remember that happening before.

The comforter on the bed was patterned with flowers in pastel shades throughout a background of pale blue. There was a table with a lamp beside the bed. On that table were several books.

Mrs. James unpacked my clothes. Every article was examined with a critical eye. The one pretty dress that I owned, and the patent leather shoes were put aside. I stood watching her and felt relief that she liked those items.

"We will keep those," she said.

The rest of my clothes were going to be discarded.

On the bed were some items, including slippers. Everything was arranged in neat rows and piles of new clothes. This was a novelty.

Previously, my clothes were secondhand. These piles of new clothes had price tags still dangling from them, waiting for me to try them on. Care had been taken, and I responded with pleasure, looking for relief and welcoming it.

"You are starting your school soon," she said, as she examined my clothes. "You will need more new clothes."

I liked that idea. I was picturing dresses for school.

As I stood watching all of this, I held onto my floppy-eared animal, gripping it closer to myself. Mrs. James started eying that animal. It was my nightly companion. My arm tightened around it when she started looking at it.

"That has to go," she said firmly, pointing at the animal.

With that, I started to cry. Mrs. James grabbed for it, but I would not let go. A tug-of-war ensued. Hysteria started to rise in me, and my protests increased in volume, which startled her in their intensity and surprised me.

I was overwhelmed with emotion, as it was hard enough for me to say goodbye to Miss Julie. That animal represented her in my mind. She was taking Miss Julie from me.

Thankfully, she sighed and let the animal go.

"We will need to give it a wash," she conceded.

That incident and the one earlier was unsettling. A stirring of uneasiness was starting to get stronger and with it, underlying fear.

Then I remember what I had been told. The medicine swallowed with the sundae.

"You cannot return to the Nest," Miss Sweet had warned.

I remembered that warning as Mrs. James continued with my makeover.

The next place of scrutiny was my hair. Mrs. James now turned to that. It was long, blonde, curly, and a struggle to untangle.

"We will get this hair cut right away."

That sounded grand to me. We moved away from unpleasantness. I was happy we were going to the hairdresser for the first time in my life. I was getting a makeover. New dresses and a new haircut.

Everything was uncertain. The lady gave me fear. The man downstairs did not cause that stirring of fear, but he kept his distance, and I felt he would remain so. He wanted peace. There was no softness in Mrs. James, just a steel determination. I was nervous and sensed I was being formed into someone else, the girl Mrs. James had wished for.

However, I came to her an orphan. That is who I was, and I was beginning to accept that. This made me different. I would be a failure at being someone else. However, I would try. I was starting to worry.

I felt like I was sitting down to an exam at school for which I was unprepared. The orphanage had helped me to accept what had happened to me.

I hope I do not fail, I thought.

Miss Julie liked me the way I was, guiding me and helping me but not with this total control. Inside, something was starting to resist. I had started to like who I was. Not trusting Mrs. James made me anxious.

Events were moving fast, and I was starting to feel I wanted to escape the car she was driving, but we were speeding ahead. I had no choice, and I could not jump out.

Miss Julie and her hugs and soft warm brown eyes were already moving far away.

Calmness did return, and later that evening, we watched a television program. We had a snack, and I read for thirty minutes, settling down with relief in my new bedroom with a book. It was *Anne of Green Gables*, which Miss Julie had given me.

Later, I would find out the television was rarely turned on. That night, we had popcorn, and I was given a bowl in a tray by my chair. That would prove to be another rare occasion, as eating in the living room was not allowed.

The next day, we went to the hair salon, and that was another first. Soon all those tangled curls were cut off, and my hair was straightened into a short bob. All I felt was relief.

Next, we were off to the seamstress to get measured for my dresses for school. The car Mrs. James was driving continued at full speed ahead, and I was just a passenger, content for the time being.

The fabric that would be used for the dresses went with us. I was hoping to see a flowered pattern.

We arrived at the house, and we were greeted by a friendly woman who ushered us into the sewing room. It was equipped with an ironing board and a chair for me to stand on so she could take my measurements. Mrs. James brought in the fabric and placed it on a table. I stepped up on the chair. As soon as she had finished, I ran over to see the fabric, anxious to see how my dresses would look.

There was no fabric with pretty flowers; instead, there was a plain dark cloth folded into a pile, which felt rough to my touch. The other pile was a lighter fabric and was white. No flowers. I stood there, puzzled. The dark fabric was itchy to the touch. Disappointment flooded me.

"Is there going to be some with flowers?" I asked.

"No flowers," Mrs. James said firmly. "You will wear a dark tunic with a white blouse."

"Is that what all the girls wear at the school?" I asked.

"I don't know. I think they should wear a tunic to school, and that is what you are wearing," she said flatly.

So, I am going to wear those ugly things in a world of flowers? I thought.

However, I kept quiet. Mrs. James's expression and tone of voice told me I would not win that battle. She was determined, and I could see the look I dreaded appear on her face. I knew when to give up.

I did not pursue it further and hoped the kids would not notice. I was different enough, and I knew kids were not kind to that.

Once those kids found out I was a foster kid, they would make fun of that. The fact that I was wearing a uniform in a school where no one wore uniforms was going to make it hard to fit in. All through my life, I tried to fit in and longed to be accepted. Would I be?

I knew I was in for a rough ride.

June at age ten on the steps of her friend Sarah's house.

Chapter 10

THE TEA PARTY

"This is not a little girl's tea party," said Mrs. James. We were standing in the kitchen, and she took me over to a cabinet in the dining room and opened a drawer. This was the next step in my education, molding me into a perfect girl. I was going to learn about tea. The ritual of making it, serving it and the proper way to drink it. It would take a girl's tea party up to a different level.

Wonderful fun, I thought.

We were going to have a grown-up tea party, which I was looking forward to.

Entering the world of tea, we visited a shop. When we stepped inside the door, the earthy scent with hints of apple and cinnamon and spices filled my nose; the ambiance of the place delighted me. Mrs. James chose carefully, and we walked away with two bags of tea.

Back at the house, Mrs. James opened the drawer in a wood cabinet. Everything in the drawer was artfully arranged. It was filled with tablecloths. The one that caught my eye was a cloth with red roses on a white background with lacy edges. It felt like silk. When I put my hand out to touch it, Mrs. James stiffened beside me, so I immediately withdrew my hand. There were small lacy white napkins in that drawer as well.

Above the drawer were sets of china cups and saucers. These were white with lacy edges.

Also in the same cabinet was a white tea pot and a sugar and cream set in the middle of a white tray. I loved it all, but they made me nervous. I was a clumsy young girl, at nine years of age. Everything looked so fragile: the pure white china and the lacy cloths.

On another shelf were some plates, the same white lacy design, and a tier for sandwiches and cakes. Every item was lovingly arranged.

Mrs. James opened another drawer, and this contained silver spoons and small knives. I was fascinated and in awe.

A tray with all these items would be brought out every afternoon as I started my training sessions. A mixture of cookies was put on a table, and the ritual began.

The table was set with one of the cloths. Mrs. James put out the candles for these occasions, and part of the ceremony was lighting these candles, which I did slowly. Small crystal glasses were placed on the table. Nervously I made my best attempt. Terrified to set everything on fire. The harder I tried, the clumsier I felt. Especially with Mrs. James standing watching me so closely.

Much care was put into the setting of the table, which was part of the lesson, as that had to be properly done.

Every detail was dealt with, and the finish was a small vase of flowers, sometimes fresh, and when fresh flowers were not available, she would use silk artificial flowers that matched the colors of the cloth. Also, the dishes were placed in their assigned spot. There were small containers of preserves when scones were served, and sometimes clotted cream was added. Mrs. James explained each item to me and the importance that each played in the ritual.

"A young British lady must always know how to serve tea," she repeated over and over.

Was I to be a young British lady? I wondered. *Better than a ward,* I concluded.

On those occasions, I would be allowed to wear a pretty dress, reserved for those teas. Two special tunics had been made of velvet with silk shirts. These dresses had been created by the same seamstress who had sewn the school uniforms. They were a surprise.

They had no flowers, but they were soft to the touch. One was a deep blue, and the other was an emerald green, intended for the teas and for church.

Mrs. James had an apron she wore for those teas. A teacup was embroidered on the apron, and she had a matching one for me.

On my feet were patent leather shoes, which completed the outfit. I could wear those shoes in the house when we served tea. For that occasion, I wore socks that had little teacups in their design, flowered with petite roses. These dress-ups were only done when we invited guests for tea.

Occasionally, Mrs. James would invite a neighborhood mom with another girl.

My physical awkwardness and my nervousness started to create a problem in the ritual. Anxiety was not helping, making it difficult not to spill the tea on those lovely cloths.

We continued the process for quite a while.

The lessons expanded to making cucumber sandwiches and sometimes, to my delight, the baking of scones. Cucumber sandwiches involved an intricate process.

The cucumbers were thinly sliced, sprinkled with a little salt, and set for a few hours to dry and crisp up in layers. Then they were carefully placed on fresh bread, always white bread and trimmed of all the crusts. Cream cheese or clotted cream would be added. The other main sandwich was smoked salmon.

The sandwiches were cut in triangles, and much care was made to keep them fresh. The prepared sandwiches were covered with a damp cloth, keeping them just moist but not soggy. These lessons remained with me. As fascinated as I was, I as also in agony. Close always to spilling or dropping.

The tea was tolerated by me with many sugar cubes, which created a syrupy drink that did not taste like tea.

The problem came with the steeping and the serving and sometimes the drinking of the beverage. Mrs. James told me I must lift my pinky finger when I put the cup to my mouth.

"Hold your pinky finger up as you put the teacup to your lips, and tip the cup gently as you drink," she instructed.

Then she would watch me intently as I attempted to do it.

This proved too difficult for me, and there were many cups that were put down in my nervousness, with tea spilling over onto those pretty cloths. The more agitated Mrs. James got, the more spills. Finally, I committed the unpardonable: I broke one of those lacy white cups. Good grief. That moment of drama happened when one of the other moms was there. Mortified again, I watched as she cleaned up the mess. The lessons were suspended. Mrs. James gave up in disgust.

To this day, I find myself lifting my pinky finger up when I drink tea.

Walking beside Mrs. James on the first day of school, one of us was happy. Wearing the itchy uniform, I looked like the perfect British schoolgirl on her way to boarding school. My blonde straight bob of hair, my dark tunic, and white blouse, with dark stockings and black shoes, created a uniform look. The problem was that I was attending a public school near our home in the east end of Toronto. It was not a private school. Mrs. James was pleased.

"You look so pretty," she cooed.

That day was a normal day at school, and no one noticed my different clothes or made remarks. I felt relief, as I wanted to fit in. I looked longingly at the pretty dresses the other girls were wearing.

No one took notice of the difference for the first week.

Every day, I was relieved to change out of those itchy tunics. They were made of wool, and I was not aware that I was allergic to wool.

I knew they made me itch, but I kept my mouth shut as itchy skin was not going to be a welcome complaint and would not be received well. Trying not to itch and attempting to keep the cloth from touching my skin was tricky. The stockings and the blouse helped. I was successful most of the time. The weather was getting cooler, so I often wore a sweater over the tunic. All this helped. How I hated those tunics, feeling very different in them and embarrassed. I was being punished. I just did not know what for.

As the days went by, the kids at school noticed. They started giggling and calling out, "Don't you have other clothes? Why do you wear the same clothes every day?"

The word got out that I was a foster kid, and the taunting increased.

"Throw-away girl. Throw-away girl," they called out to me as I walked near them in the halls and outside at recess.

Wearing a uniform every day in a school that did not require uniforms, it was impossible to fit in. School became a torment. They were lonely days. The one bright light was the classes. I kept quiet about the taunting, but I was miserable.

I buried myself in books.

One day, walking alone after school and feeling discouraged, my thoughts were on what I would do when I got home. I hoped Mrs. James would allow me to listen to a radio program, as the television was rarely allowed.

Deep into my own thoughts, I did not notice a girl had come along beside me.

"Hi," she said.

"Hi," I replied, surprised.

Beside me was a girl walking astride a red bicycle. She looked like Anne of Green Gables. Long curly red hair and a face full of freckles and mischievous green eyes. Looking at her, I felt my heart lift, as if someone had removed the weights.

"You live on my street," she said. "Do you want to play some games with me?"

We continued walking home and parted when we reached my house. I discovered that she was my neighbor.

"I will have to go home first and get permission," I said. "I will try and come to you after supper."

I watched her walk a little farther to her home, and we waved at each other. To my surprise, her home was visible from my house.

Her name was Sarah, and we became fast friends. Like me, she was an outsider. Unlike me, she was tough. Her mom was divorced. She had been shamed at school.

The kids did not bully her like me, but they did not befriend her. She was too tough to be bullied and did not seem to care that they excluded her.

Sarah was an athlete and strong. I was small and nowhere close to an athlete. I was a bookworm, clumsy physically and not into sports, unless they were forced on me. Especially competitive sports, as I retreated into a shell at the hint of competition.

Sarah started joining me on our walks home from school. Her red bike was always with her. We played with each other at recess.

When she was around me, the taunting stopped. We were not included, but she did not care. I started not to care too. Finally, I had a friend. That changed everything for me.

I found myself laughing. Darkness and fear left my heart. The quietness in the house I went home to every day had been filling me with despair.

With Sarah in my life, it became bearable. I was not the girl Mrs. James wanted. Hard as I tried, I could not be her. We were both disappointed when I tried but failed miserably at being that girl.

"Can I play with Sarah after school?" I asked Mrs. James one night.

We were doing the dishes after supper.

"Sarah does not have a father," she said bluntly. "Her mother is divorced."

She rubbed one of the dishes vigorously. I paused in drying the dish in my hand.

"What is divorced?" I asked.

She stopped and looked at me and then gave me an explanation I did not understand. Her face registered disgust. I had heard that Sarah's father had left her mother. Was that her crime? I did not understand that.

"You can play outside with Sarah after school, but you cannot go inside the house," she said firmly. "You will get sick if you sit on their toilet."

She went on to explain that Sarah's mom was filthy.

Did divorce make people dirty? I wondered.

I did not ask any more questions. All I cared about at that point was that she was going to let me play with Sarah.

As the days went by and headed for summer, Sarah and I were together every chance we could. Sometimes, the other kids in the neighborhood allowed us to play hide-and-seek with them in the warmer evenings; we'd play until the streetlights came on.

As we caught the last light of the day, we came alive, hiding behind trees and sneaking into the back yards of the neighbor's homes. We were full of energy and the joy of the days of spring. It was a time of happiness for me.

I got my first crush on a boy that summer. He kissed me once when we were playing hide-and-seek. Just a quick kiss. Chaste and fast, catching me off guard. He was my first crush, and his little face became my dream boy. One quick kiss did it.

It was a secret, and I treasured it.

At the end of the street was a bit of green space next to the railway tracks. Sarah and I would try to catch butterflies there among the wildflowers. As they hovered over a wildflower, we got close but never caught one. The lovely monarchs reminded me of little fairies, and I thought they were magical. Those days were full of joy and freedom.

One day, nature had its way, and I had to rush into Sarah's home and use her washroom. I was nervous about the germs Mrs. James had warned me about. I tried not sitting down on the toilet seat.

I used my hands on either side of the seat and held myself up. Sarah watched giggling from the doorway.

"Why are you doing that?" she asked.

"I don't want to touch the toilet."

Finally, the both of us broke down in laughter because neither of us could make any sense of it. Landing down with a plunk on the toilet seat ended that whole affair.

We had much fun over that, and I got a lot of teasing, especially when I explained to Sarah the reason for all the nonsense. Her house was not dirty, but I wondered if I'd get sick.

However, as the days went by, and I did not get sick, then I started to realize how silly it all was. Sarah's house was not spotless, but it was clean. Their house could not be clean as mine. We hardly lived in that house. We walked around in tiptoe. We lived in a hushed house, devoid of germs. Devoid of life.

Meeting Sarah's mom was refreshing. She was warm and friendly. Again, I could not understand what the fuss was about her. She was kind to me. Surprisingly, Sarah and her mom both knew they were regarded as outsiders, but they were not concerned. They shared their own secret that foolish people did not know. They were amused by it all. It gave them strength, and I wished I could be like them.

They both knew I was an orphan and understood my situation with Mrs. James, although we did not discuss it. Whenever I visited the house, I was welcomed. This comforted me, and I began to feel like a member of their family.

Forbidden fruit beckoned me. Sarah's bike was the same color as the apple. Mrs. James had given me many warnings about that bike.

However, like the apple, red and enticing, on the other side of the fence, I wanted to ride the bike. Longing filled my heart when I looked at it, which came with a warning:

"The streets are too busy with cars, and it is too dangerous."

This warning rang false with me, as we lived on a quiet residential street. Our street was a dead end, with a field and train tracks at the end of it.

I pleaded with her to no avail, and when I did that, she emphasized her point. We were having a conversation, so we were once again doing the dishes. Our meals were quiet, and any talk tended to happen when we did the dishes. That day, she turned to me and gave me a warning.

"Stay off of Sarah's bike."

I backed off because that order was accompanied by the look, which made me fearful. It was a scathing look because she did not like me in those days. Mr. James looked up from the table and gave me a look of warning when he heard her. She sounded angry.

Her dislike of me and her hostility was turning to hatred. I did not persist about the bike. I did not feel she was being honest. I felt that depriving me of that pleasure had nothing to do with my safety. Kids just rode bikes. It felt cruel.

The house had become the place where I slept and ate. Everything was orderly and efficient, and I could have set my clock by the meals and the routine in the quiet, cold house. There was a strange quietness that did not bring peace with it. There was too much tension in the quietness.

The meals were similar. Grilled cheese sandwiches and soft-boiled eggs and soup were the lunches. The suppers did not vary from week to week. The meals were always on time, always the same. I could tell which day it was by the suppers.

No clutter was allowed in the house. Mrs. James smoked at the same time each day. There was a drawer in the kitchen where she kept her cigarettes and lighter.

Looking at them in her drawer, I resisted the temptation to try one. The neatness of the package and the lighter assumed their own space. Did she create a square in the drawer where she set them in the middle of? This fascinated me, and I often checked to see if it varied. It did not.

Opening the drawer, I was tempted to move the order around but resisted the urge. One time when I was standing in front of the open drawer, Mr. James came up behind me.

"Better not," he said quietly.

I heeded his warning.

There were no surprises in that house. Like a graveyard.

Little girls do not belong in a graveyard.

In the morning, Mrs. James would appear from her bedroom with her makeup and jewelry in place.

Her husband was rarely seen, and whenever he was home, he was either reading or listening to the radio. Sometimes, I would see him on the back porch, reading the newspaper and smoking his pipe. He was in the background.

Mrs. James was the dominant personality, and he made his own way of peace. He kept to his corner of the world.

Escaping every chance I could manage, I found reasons to leave the house. Occasionally, on rainy days, Mrs. James would allow Sarah and me to play board games in the basement. I was usually with Sarah at her house.

The television remained dark and mute. Whenever it was turned on, it was scheduled and planned for. On a Sunday evening, the neighbors would get together and watch *The Ed Sullivan Show*.

The radio had more space in my life. Sarah and I often listened to *Little Orphan Annie* and *The Shadow*: "Who knows what evil lurks in the hearts of men? The Shadow knows!" I had to be torn away from the radio, especially before Sarah entered my life.

Few conversations went on between Mrs. James and me, and there was silence at the dinner table. The phrase "Silence is deafening" was true in that house.

Back then, the Canadian Adoption Service (CAS) insisted that foster parents take their children to church.

Off we trotted to church every Sunday. We did not say grace before meals, and faith was not evident in the house. I did not like church, bone dry. The only beauty I saw was the stained-glass windows. Willingly distracted by the sun hitting them, I would look for that to endure the long formal services.

The other distraction was the organ, accompanied by the piano and singing the old hymns, helping to make the time tolerable. Mr. and Mrs. James dutifully took me every Sunday, but there was no joy in that task. It was something we got through. We went and left with rare exchanges with anyone else. We shook hands with the minister on the way out the front door, and that was the extent of contact with the other congregants.

It was quite different from the chapel at the orphanage. It was a formal church and was joyless after my experience at the Salvation Army orphanage, dry and boring. There was little singing, and there was no band. I did not see my imaginary dad. If he were there, he was so formal I could not imagine children climbing up on his lap or playing around him. I had not forgotten that dad, but he seemed distant and far away, lost in the coldness.

Impatient to spend my Sunday afternoons with Sarah, we made it home, and I changed quickly; when we were finished our lunch, I was on my way to her house.

The red bike continued to assume giant proportions in my mind, a huge temptation. I looked at it with longing as Sarah sailed past on it.

She knew all the tricks and would let her hands go and sail down the hill with her red hair blowing in the wind.

Was I remembering the dreams of Lady Godiva? Not on a horse but on a bike?

I coveted that bike. Sarah had a horn, and she would honk it at me as she sailed by, tempting me. The bike had red ribbons that also sailed in the wind.

Sarah and I were different. I had blonde hair and hazel eyes that turned different colors with my moods. Mrs. James told me they turned black sometimes. That gave me the willies.

Standing in front of the mirror, I would try and make them go black. I was relieved they did not turn black. I did not want to have eyes that turned black.

Sarah was tall, and I was petite. To my eyes, she was stunning. She was strong in a way that I was not. Hurt by the comments and taunting of the kids, I would ruminate on them. Sarah did not care what people thought. I cared too much.

When I expressed my hurt and repeated their words, Sarah would shrug her shoulders. She would scoff at them, which was good for me.

Her mom was soft and kind but strong like Sarah in a way that I had not known a woman to be. She was attractive, and I could see Sarah got her beauty from her mom, who had that beautiful hair and eyes. She also had a sprinkling of freckles across the bridge of her nose and on her cheeks. I loved the freckles and wished I had some. Both Sarah and her mom had a happy relationship. I envied Sarah that she had a wonderful mom. They laughed together. There was a good deal of laughter in that house.

Both Sarah and I loved a delightful story and adventure. I was a reader and shared some of my stories with her, and we both listened to the radio. There was no silent television in Sarah's home. They did not have television, but we did not miss it, as we were always busy at something.

We were two conspirators sharing a secret: I began riding my friend's bike. My days became exciting as I started taking turns with Sarah on the bike. The days rolled by, and I became complacent.

Loosening some restraints, I was becoming less careful. Our street had a decline, and on the bike, we could take our feet off the pedals and sail with the wind.

This would take me right past my house, so I had avoided that route, but Sarah egged me on. I overcame my fear and pedaled up the incline past my house; as I did not see the car in the driveway, I thought I was safe.

On the way down on the decline, she was standing on our front step with her arms folded across her chest. I felt her anger coming at me in waves, and my heart was filled with dread.

She shouted at me, "June, stop! Get off that bike."

My stomach turned over, and I felt suddenly sick.

Sarah had disappeared. Probably scared too. She was gone from where she had been standing. I did not blame her one bit. All I saw was her back, running away. She did not stop for her bike.

Mrs. James ran down the driveway, waving her hands at me and shouting. I stopped suddenly, terrified of her. She ran towards me in the road. I put my foot on the brake and dismounted. She ran up to me, grabbed the red bike, and marched away with it.

"Get back to the house," she growled at me in a voice I barely recognized.

When Mrs. James grabbed the bike, she was so angry, she was shaking. I ran into the house, craning my neck trying to see Sarah.

Mrs. James was walking with long strides, and both her hands were on the bike, calling out to Sarah to stop. The culprit she was running after was not slowing down, either. Sarah had run into her house.

There was no Sarah in sight. It was a windy day, and Mrs.

James's manicured hair was blowing in the wind, and that hair just made the whole scene wild. The shouting and the running and intense emotion swirled around Mrs. James. We were all in trouble.

I ran quickly into the house and went up to my room; I sat down on my bed and looked down at my shoes, which in my haste I had forgotten to remove. I took them off and stuffed them under the bed. I picked up my floppy-eared friend and started rocking myself.

Chapter 11

CONSEQUENCES

My bike riding days ended.

Sarah, and her bike, disappeared from my life. My pretend family was gone. Mrs. James suspended all my privileges, and the silence in the house was deep, like a grave.

At night, in that house, I cried, afraid and grieving the loss of my friend.

Tossing and turning, unable to sleep with a headache from crying, I wanted to shut out my grief. I went to the washroom, opened the medicine cabinet, and shook out two pills from a bottle. Mrs. James took those pills when she had a headache.

The pills helped me to fall asleep. I discovered for the first time the temporary relief of pills, which threw a warm blanket over my pain. When I broke out in an itchy rash, I suspected the pills were the cause, as I started to take them every night. At the age of ten, I was experiencing the draw of something to ease my pain.

One night, I took four and promptly threw them up. After that, I stopped taking them, and my rash disappeared, along with the pills.

Food was turning to cement in my stomach, as the silent mealtimes were deadly.

The dinner table remained mute. I tried chatting away, due to my nervousness. The sound of my own voice was better than silence, I thought.

The stillness magnified the sounds of chewing, and the clinking of the cutlery on plates echoed in the room. Soft sounds of slurping became embarrassing and too loud.

One mealtime, Mr. James removed his false teeth at the table. Something got stuck, and he took out the dentures and picked them clean. He had forgotten he had an audience, and Mrs. James and I stopped eating and stared at him, me with curiosity and Mrs. James with disgust.

Mr. James came out of his stupor and realized we were staring at him, and his face went red as he remembered he was not alone. He often brought the newspaper to the table and absorbed himself in it.

Our breathing was loud in the silence. The odd cough was startling and echoed in the quietness. Sounds that I was never aware of seemed to speak their own language. I had the irresistible urge to start giggling, especially when Mr. James took out his teeth. It would have been like laughing at a funeral. Fortunately, I restrained the impulse.

It was a time of tension. The effort to avoid contact was exhausting for all of us.

The final week of school approached, and when I went home on the last day, I left my slacks behind.

I realized this when we were sitting at the silent table, having our supper. Forgetting my slacks was important.

"I forgot my slacks at school," I blurted out in the silence.

My voice sounded loud, and even to my ears, it sounded like a shout. Everyone jerked.

Mrs. James immediately put her fork down with what sounded like a crash that echoed in the silent room. Mr. James put his paper down, and the two of them looked at me with mutual dislike. Unfortunately, I had forgotten my slacks before, and there had been a series of lectures. My mind was often in the clouds.

"Run back to school and get those slacks. If you do not return with them, Mr. James will give you a spanking.

The word that screamed at me was *spanking*. Even though I could not imagine mild-mannered Mr. James spanking me, I thought he might do it. Looking over at him when she said that, I was surprised when he simply lowered his head back to his paper. He appeared angry, and I was scared. I had never seen him angry. We were all falling apart.

Sweet, mild-mannered Mr. James angry? That thought had me scared.

I got up from the table and ran out the door. It was an early summer evening, and the school was closed, but I ran. No one would be there, and then what?

Running with my heart beating in my ears and my legs pumping as hard as I could make them, I was hoping that a miracle would happen, and someone would be at the school.

As I drew closer to the school, I could see it was empty. No cars in the parking lot, no kids. This was the last weekend of June, and the school had emptied out for the summer several hours ago. I still walked around the building and tried some of the doors. It was futile.

Could I return to that house of hate?

Standing there in the empty parking lot, I was undecided. With a sinking heart, every choice was grim. Approaching my tenth birthday, I did not belong anywhere. There was no safety for me, as I was unloved. I stood in that parking lot on that beautiful day and knew I could not go back to that house.

I wandered to a nearby park, where I stood and watched the other children play, wishing I could simply be free to play too. My choices were limited. Knowing I could not return to that cold, angry house, and the possibility of a beating.

I had shorts and a T-shirt on, and the day was becoming cool. Hesitating and uncertain, I shivered and felt lost. I was desperate and alone; there was no one to reach out to for help. Where would I eat? Where would I sleep? I did not know. I was afraid and confused.

There was no safety anywhere for me. I saw a man sitting on a bench, staring at me, and I knew I was drawing unwelcome attention. I was frightened and aware of my vulnerability.

At the edge of the park were several bikes the kids had tossed in a pile. I walked over to the bikes and stood there. The bikes were tempting but stealing someone's bike was never an option for me.

The moments I stood there stretched, and time stood still for me as I watched the children play. Lost in indecision.

A car pulled up to the curb and stopped suddenly, with the wheels screeching. I looked over and saw Mrs. James walk quickly around her car towards me. My instinct was to run, but she caught me as I was turning; she grabbed my arm and walked me quickly back to the car. She opened the door to the back seat and pushed me in. She had solved my dilemma. I was not going anywhere. Trembling with fear, I sat in the car.

She drove to a street near our home and pulled up to a red brick bungalow I was not familiar with. She stopped the car, came around to the back, and opened the door.

I got out, and she guided me firmly around the side of the house to the door. She pulled out a key and opened the door, and we went inside. We walked down the stairs to a room in the basement; she stood back and nudged me inside the room. Everything was done in quick jerky movements that displayed her silent anger. She spoke two words.

"Wait here," she said.

She turned and left, locking the door behind her.

I looked around at the small room. Relieved, but puzzled, I sat down on a sofa under a basement window. Relieved, because I was not being taken back to that silent house.

I expected this was a drop-off point, and the lady with the sundaes would fetch me.

Listening with my ear against the door, I heard Mrs. James talking to the neighbor upstairs. I could not make out their muffled voices through the door. The words were not clear, but I could discern the tones of voices. Mrs. James's voice was shrill and angry; it gave me chills. The other voice was softer, murmuring in a soothing tone. The voice of a woman. I had no idea what was going on.

I heard the door upstairs open and close and then silence.

There was a pillow and blanket on the sofa; I waited for the woman with the sundaes.

Hearing steps coming down the stairs, I stood up, getting prepared to leave with Miss Sweet. However, it was Mrs. James who returned. She unlocked the door and said two words:

"Sit. Stay."

Obediently, I sat back down on the sofa.

Moving quickly and efficiently but with the same angry jerky movements, she brought in everything I owned, including my toy box.

She did this, slapping things on the floor. Quickly and efficiently. Not saying a word while I sat and watched her. She was not looking at me, keeping her head turned away.

Turning around abruptly, she left.

Looking around, I could see a washroom through a door. Other than a sofa, the room had only a table, on which there was some snack food, drinks, and a lamp. Preparation had been made for me, which told me I would be there for a while. That alarmed me.

I opened the lid of my toy box, and the contents gave me comfort, relieved to see my stuffed animal and my books. Thankful, I pulled out my animal and a book.

I stood up on the sofa, stretched up, and looked out the window into a yard. It looked empty and forlorn in the twilight. My situation was becoming unclear. The coldness was getting worse as the sun was starting to set. I remembered what it was like to be cold, how it brought with it a sense of loneliness. I looked at the food on the table.

I unwrapped a sandwich and some potato chips and ate them and a chocolate bar. Comforted by the food, I went into the washroom and checked to see if there were any pills. It was good there were none. I would have taken them for sure. Pills had offered me comfort before. There would have been no hesitation to swallow any pills that may have been there. I did not have a conscious suicidal wish. The blankety feeling they offered was what I was looking for.

I heard people moving about upstairs and the sound of children's voices.

As the hours dragged by, I grew more confused.

What is happening to me? I wondered. *Is this a further punishment?*

I clung to my stuffed animal and picked up a book to distract myself.

One day, I was sailing down the street on a red bike, and now here I was.

The sounds of people moving around upstairs penetrated through the ceiling of the room, but I had no idea who those people were. Calling out was not a good idea.

Who were these people? I could hear voices of children coming through the ceiling. I was in a state of confusion as the hours dragged by.

Reading was impossible for me, as my mind could not focus. I was starting to shake with cold and fear.

This started with inner trembling, and then my body would shake; it felt like a tornado that was impossible to control. Wrapping my arms around myself, I would try and make it stop. However, it had its own life. My inner voice was speaking to me.

No one came, and the room darkened as night approached.

Curling up on the sofa, I hugged my floppy-eared friend to me and finally fell asleep. I forced my mind to focus on better times, on those dreamy days with Sarah and a little boy who gave me a butterfly kiss.

No one said a word to me on that long weekend. Was I going to be there forever? My eternal punishment? I did not know. Food appeared in the morning, consisting of cheese and crackers and sometimes a sandwich. I did not eat much of it because my appetite was stilled by fear. When I tried to eat, I felt nauseous.

Did the neighbors know how long I would be there?

In my mind, the people upstairs became part of a plot and party to the cause of my suffering, so I was afraid to call out to them.

Even pleasant, mild Mr. James turned into someone I did not know.

I slept a lot, curled into a ball on the sofa in a fetal position, trying to keep warm. On other occasions, I filled my mind with fantasies and imaginations, trying to place myself in another world. I kept standing on the sofa, trying to figure a way out. Nothing changed as I repeatedly did that, but I needed to keep checking, hoping I would see someone.

The hours dragged on.

Chapter 12

A SPOONFUL OF SUGAR

Finally, after long, empty hours, the door was unlocked, and a flustered Miss Sweet entered. The usually calm and efficient woman seemed fearful and anxious.

I fell into her arms with relief; she held me while I shook and cried. In her arms, the shaking now took full flight We both stood there for a few moments because I was so distraught, I could barely walk.

Miss Sweet and I gathered my possessions together, and we quickly exited the basement. She picked up the toy box, and I carried the rest. The people upstairs remained mysterious. They did not appear as we made our hurried exit.

Placing everything in the trunk of the car, I opened the door and sat in the back seat. The ride was silent in the short drive. Both of us were shocked.

Miss Sweet drove to a restaurant. We left the car and went inside. It was close to midday, and people had gathered for lunch.

I was served my first hot meal in days. That hamburger and fries tasted like heaven, and I savored each bite. The food brought with it a sense of sanity. I wasn't aware how hungry I was until I bit into that hamburger and put the first ketchup-dipped fry into my mouth. I was free and alive. As we ate the first course, we were absorbed in the meal, and conversation remained limited to the ordering of food and silently eating. I focused on the sensory satisfaction of the food and was content for the time.

Miss Sweet left for a few minutes, first to the washroom and then over to the pay phones; the first part of the meal was uneventful.

I was happy to watch life around me, with the busy servers moving from table to table, taking orders and delivering food. The activity around me gave me comfort, restoring a sense of wellbeing. Miss Sweet returned to the table.

Next came our treat: the ritual butterscotch sundae, Miss Sweet's favorite dish. Through all the trouble ahead, they remained the go-to treat. I carefully removed the cherry and put it on the side of the dish to savor it at the very last. My hands still had a slight tremor, but I was recovering. Still, the distant cold hatred I had encountered had left me shaken.

The taste of ice cream and the sweetness did their magic.

For the moment, I felt safe.

I was listening to Miss Sweet, determined and ever efficient, preparing me for what lay ahead.

Sitting at the table across from her, I watched her mouth; her face was moving away from me. Her brief show of sympathy was gone. My momentary relief and feeling of safety also were gone as I listened intently to her words.

Leaning forward in my seat, my sundae was beginning to melt as her words were distracting me from eating.

Miss Sweet was also leaning forward, waving her arms around, emphasizing her words, spoken in a firm, cold tone. This shoved away the brief comfort I was enjoying from the food and my escape from the basement. My relief was turning to alarm. I did not trust this woman with her butterscotch sundaes.

As she spoke, she continued to spoon the syrupy goodness into her mouth, speaking between mouthfuls.

The threat of her words remained separated from the sweetness of the sundae. It was a sinister contrast. My spoon was halfway to my mouth, frozen in the middle of motion, as I listened to her.

"You must not run away again," she said, warning me with a firm voice. "If you do, you will be considered a juvenile delinquent and will have to go to a training school.

She considered there was nothing, simply nothing that would be a reason to run away. I wondered what these people would do if someone killed me.

What if someone murdered me? They would do nothing. They would blame me for getting murdered.

My thoughts ran around in a circle. I was in a maze, wandering around, looking for a way out. Feeling lost and confused. Things were taking an ugly turn. I was afraid what I would find at the end of that maze. Would it lead me to something worse?

I knew I was powerless. That reality flooded my brain with a sick, dark feeling in the pit of my stomach. This was the truth of my life, a truth I was powerless to stop.

I was in the middle of my own nightmare, and this woman sitting before me was telling me there was no escape. The horror of what she was doing was made clear as she continued to eat her sundae and talked; she clearly relished the dessert, totally distanced from me.

I had stopped eating, and my sundae was melting. She was blandly threatening me. The sundae drew more of her attention than my reaction. Her total indifference was frightening.

I had a sense of entrapment, like looking for a way out of the basement. There was no way out. I had a brain. I would need to use it because I sensed more trouble was coming.

Being locked into a stranger's basement was in the past. We were moving ahead, into what? Miss Sweet's eyes had a bland, unflinching look that I was starting to know. The emptiness of it gave me the sense that she did not see me. Instead, her vision was filled with her own agenda, blocking me out. There was no expression in her eyes, and she was not smiling. I knew that being a juvenile delinquent was not a good thing.

How could I go from a failed perfect girl to that? It was the first time I had heard the term. I was ten years old, a very young girl to be carrying such a label.

She proceeded to give me an ultimatum. The restaurant was busy around us, but the noises were dimmed, and all I heard were her words.

She went on to describe the place we were going to in glowing terms. Wanting to believe her, I felt the underlining threat of her words. My own sundae had melted, but Miss Sweet spooned the remaining part of her sundae into her mouth. I was expecting her to lift the dish up and lick it dry. Her obvious enjoyment of the sundae while she talked was not in harmony with the words she was saying. She finally finished and licked the spoon with satisfaction. Her ability to do that increased my horror. The contrast strengthened the threat of her words.

"No one got hurt, right? It was simply a misunderstanding."

The misunderstanding she was talking about was the gap between Mrs. James asking the CAS to pick me up and their inability to do so until the end of the long weekend.

Because of her anger, Mrs. James had dumped me in a stranger's basement until they did so.

The cruelty of a young girl locked into a stranger's basement over those long days had already been rationalized away, and now she wanted to move me on from that cruelty. There was a mix-up, and no way was she going to take responsibility for it. It would rest on my own shoulders.

"You should not have run away. If you keep running away, we will send you to a training school."

She went on with her description of where we were heading next. She leaned forward convincingly, saying things about the new place that left me wary.

"They are a lovely family and have other children; you are lucky to have this chance."

I knew I had no choice, but my thoughts were my own. I would hide them. Another birthday was close. Soon I would be eleven years old, and I was starting to accept the reality of my situation. Nothing made sense in the Alice in Wonderland world I was in. Could I do this thing until I grew up? Until I got out from under these people who were shunting me around? At least try and stay alive until I was free to walk away? These were the questions I was asking myself.

I sat before her, nodding my head and remaining silent.

The message was clear:

Make it work.

Chapter 13

THE YEARS OF THE LOCUSTS

> What the palmerworm has left, the locusts eat.
> (Joel 1:4 NIV)

Miss Sweet and I walked up three steps that led to the front door of a semidetached house in Toronto's east end, known today as the Beaches. It was a plain brown brick house with a small front porch. It was the beginning of summer and a beautiful day, but I did not take much notice of it.

Miss Sweet knocked on the door, and we were let in. I was left in the front room, and Miss Sweet and the woman who let us in left me alone for a few minutes. I stood and looked around at what would be my new home. Every nerve in me was hyper vigilant, taking in the place. Danger had made me look for any signs that would help me to know what I was walking into. Strength to survive would come within myself. This was a tough lesson, but I needed to learn it.

The house felt chilly, and I was glad for the sweater I was wearing. The room was long and narrow. The color on the walls was a shade of musky green. My first sense was darkness. The house smelled old and dusty. Unlike Mrs. James's home, this place was worn and cluttered. Heavy old furniture assumed space and created a crowded room. A television was on but muted. It was the lonely light in the dark room. The room was dark because the front porch shaded the only window where natural light would come in.

I could see through the hall that the dining room was adjacent to the living room, and the doorway to the kitchen was through the dining room. As I completed my perusal, the family and Miss Sweet entered the room.

Mrs. Haney, the foster mother, was a large robust woman in her mid-forties. Her flushed face had a wide welcoming smile.

"So glad you are here," she boomed.

Unlike Mrs. James, she did not attempt a hug, and I was happy for that. Instead, she stepped forward and held out her hand, and I shook it. She was a big woman. Her hair was permed in short curls, and she wore glasses. Her mouth was wide with her smile. She had a round face. Although she was smiling, I could not discern warmth in her eyes. Looking into eyes was always one of the first things I did. Eyes spoke to me. Hers told me nothing. They frightened me in their emptiness. That big smile did not reach her eyes. She was assessing me with them. I felt their warning. The stirring of the rest of the family around her drew my attention away.

Each member of the family stepped forward as they were introduced to me.

Mr. Haney, a wiry balding man, wore glasses. He appeared pale and greeted me quietly in a voice barely louder than a whisper, his head bowed. To me, he appeared weak and submissive. He did not meet my eyes and kept his head slightly lower.

A heavyset girl who looked about fifteen came forward in a zombie-like shuffle. She barely raised her head and moved in a lifeless way. Lucie was a stocky girl dressed in a shapeless brown dress. Her hair had short tight brown curls.

"This is Lucie," said Mrs. Haney.

Lucie, another foster child, nodded, but neither one of us connected. I sensed something wrong, something off.

"Lucie is very shy," Mrs. Haney said quickly.

As I was introduced to each member of the family, I assessed them in my mind with the same question: *Are they safe or unsafe?*

Two boys were introduced next. First was Richard, who we called Rick; he was fourteen years old and thin as a broomstick; acne covered his face. There was a sneakiness about him that made my skin crawl.

He also looked surly. Barely acknowledging the introduction, he looked me up and down insolently, not even attempting to hide his examination. He repulsed me. I did not enjoy this kind of attention from a boy.

Be careful of this boy, I thought.

The younger boy, Albert, whom we called Al, appeared to be a normal eleven-year-old. He was plump and wore glasses and appeared cheerful and open. He was the most likeable person in the room. He greeted me with a smile.

I sensed I would be safe with him.

Miss Sweet said her goodbyes and exited quickly after giving me a brief hug. I felt her relief. As she left, she shot me a look that I understood as a warning. Her eyes flashed that message, and I read it.

Lucie took me upstairs to our room. We did not have much to carry as I was told I could not take up my toy box because it was too big for the bedroom.

The toy box disappeared to the basement, and I did not see it again. Following Lucie up the stairs, I sensed her avoidance. We walked down a long hall that led to the front of the house on the upper level. The atmosphere of the house changed, and I shivered.

I managed to hold on to my stuffed floppy-eared animal. When Lucie showed me the top bunk that I would be sleeping in, I quickly hid it under the pillow. I sensed if I did not hide it, I would lose it. Lucie watched me do that and nodded at me with approval. A very slight nod but discernable in the semi-dark room.

I would be sleeping on the top bunk in the narrow room, with one small window. Lucie did not say anything but showed me the bed I would sleep in. There was one dresser, and she opened two empty drawers and indicated I could use them.

There was one cupboard, and I hung up the few clothes I had and put my other clothes away while Lucie watched silently. There was no lamp in the room, and I wondered where I would read. The room did not encourage a reader. Books were not seen so far. Already, I sensed this was not a house where readers lived. I would have to find a way.

A large room had been divided to make two bedrooms. Al slept on the other side of the partition. Rick had his bedroom at the other end of the hall, and Mr. and Mrs. Haney were in the middle of the two bedrooms. I was glad Rick was at the other end. I would not want to sleep near that boy.

The second floor had little natural light, and the walls were painted neutral colors. No pictures or décor broke up the darkness.

In the first few weeks, the house was quiet, and I went along with the routine. Lucie remained distant and hard to get to know.

Our conversations were only about the logistics of living together; she did not welcome anything personal. I was encouraging her to feel safe with me. I sensed her fear and had sympathy for whatever was making her so reserved and cautious.

She was not a mean girl, and in fact, I sensed kindness. Her brown eyes often told me that in unguarded moments. However, she was careful and distant.

The television was on constantly, and the family gathered in the living room several hours a day. Mrs. Haney liked soap operas. I was enjoying this new form of entertainment.

Everyone lived in their own worlds, and personal conversations did not happen, even at mealtimes. Occasionally, we would play canasta or Monopoly on the front porch on those long summer days. Allowed to go for walks, I would grab a book, take the long walk to the lake, and find a place to sit. Walking and playing board games were good days in that time. We attended another boring church every Sunday. That church was a little less formal than the one I had attended at the James's.

The only time the kids relaxed was around the television and when we played games on the front porch.

I found a reading spot in the dining room. I usually had the spot to myself. The remainder of that first summer was pleasant. Mrs. Haney allowed me to join the local library, which was within walking distance to the house. In inclement weather, I often went there and sat inside. Still, it was a lonely time, and the house seemed to be walking on eggshells, waiting for something. Tension walked in that house.

I was into my twelfth year, and I could feel my body changing. Inside of me, a young woman was emerging. Growing up was happening, and I was also a girl in waiting for the day I could free myself from what I felt was the snare of the fowler. Nowhere felt safe for me. I tried to keep my head down and wait out the years ahead until the day I could support myself. I had my dreams. However, I sensed there was further danger ahead for me. I hoped I would survive those years.

One day, toward the end of summer, Mrs. Haney brought me upstairs to the bedroom. I followed her heavy, slow steps up the stairs. She was carrying a pile of garments. Mrs. Haney was a seamstress, and she worked at her sewing machine during the days. She was able to earn a little money that way, as she was skillful and made dresses for weddings.

Until that day, Mrs. Haney and I had few exchanges. Rules had been set up, and all of us followed them. They were well established, and if I had questions, I asked Lucie. I did not know Mrs. Haney. She was a formidable presence in the house but distant. Mr. Haney was a shadow. I avoided Rick as much as I could. Lucie and Al were the only people in the house I connected with. Mrs. Haney scared me.

"School will be starting soon, and we need to go through your clothes."

I stood in the bedroom, and she walked around me and set the piles of garments on the bed.

My heart stilled.

Mrs. Haney sat down heavily on the lower bunk, and she pulled out dresses that were in the pile of garments. They would have been better for Lucie, who was heavier and taller than me. Trying one on, I was dismayed that it was two sizes too large and hung on my small frame like a sack and went down to my ankles. I looked down in disbelief at the length and the bulk of the dress. I disappeared in it. The color was brown.

Mrs. Haney had made the shapeless dresses from a heavy material. Two others were the same size but in a lighter material. They were functional but ugly dresses. Not intended to enhance but to distract beauty.

Mrs. Haney watched to see my reaction. However, I was getting smarter. Somehow, it felt like a trap. Waiting for a reaction and ready to pounce.

There was no protest from me. I stood there mutely, nodding.

I knew this was not a woman to argue with. Taking my cue from everyone in the house, I was not that foolish. I was already afraid of her. Those clothes would be my new uniform, different from the tunics that caused me to itch, but the purpose behind them was the same.

The person I was, my own identity, would be hidden behind those dresses.

The emerging comeliness of a young woman was to be buried beneath those ugly dresses. What she did not realize was that she would try, but she could not bury nature. I knew that clothes could not do that. However, that was the purpose. I said nothing.

I was also waiting. My time would come.

Two nice dresses appeared, and my spirit rose at the sight of them. Those two nice dresses were for show and would rarely be worn. I tried them on, and they fit me perfectly. Unlike the ugly dresses, they enhanced beauty. One was a black crepe with raised white polka dots and a white collar. That dress delighted me, and I saw Mrs. Haney scowl with anger.

"Put them aside, and you will not wear them. I will tell you when you can."

I nodded my head. Normal clothes for play were allowed, such as shorts and slacks, so she did not discard those.

She pointed to the drab dresses that were too large for me.

"You will wear those to school."

I was thankful my stuffed animal was hidden from her view. She had forgotten about it. Lucie and I changed our own bedding, so it was a good place to hide it. I knew she would never let me keep it should she remember.

Now she turned to my hair. Mrs. James had cut and straightened my hair. Mrs. Haney decided she would put a perm in it. My hair had started to show its own waves. Nature had its way.

"Your hair is too straight; we are going to put a perm in it."

One woman wanted straight, and the other one wanted curly. This whole business of hair was confusing. What was this thing about hair?

She sat on the bed and handed me some black, heavy cotton leotards. After I put everything on, I was a caricature of an orphan.

The clothes were long and baggy on my small frame. I could pull the heavy stockings up and fold them over at my waist, they were so big for me. Large glasses and soon a permed ball of hair would complete the look. I was also given a pair of laced-up shoes that were functional but ugly.

Will I be able to make friends? Is this why Lucie looks the way she does?

Mrs. Haney left me to put the clothes away and told me to join her in the kitchen. There she proceeded with the process of perming my hair. The strong smell of the chemicals she was using gave me a headache. Also, the tightness of the rollers caused the entire process to be painful, with my eyes tearing up at the smell. It felt like a punishment. She rolled up tight rollers, and I sat for some time with the chemicals on my hair.

Finally, she rinsed my hair, and I had the same tight curls as Lucie. At eleven years of age, I had a perm. This lady was on a mission. The mission was to destroy prior to school any visage of beauty and to create ugly (or at least try).

She held up a mirror with satisfaction, and I looked at myself and tried to hold back my tears. For the moment, I thought ugly had won.

However, once again, as Mrs. Haney stared at me with those empty eyes, watching me intently for a reaction, I gave her a feeble smile and nodded. She walked away, and I stifled my tears, knowing she had achieved her purpose. However, I was about survival.

For the time, I was buried in the relentless hands of this woman, but I was still breathing, and I would wait. My time would come.

"Don't make a fuss," Lucie whispered to me when we were alone in our room that night.

I felt Lucie's agitation and panic. As her fear mounted, I submitted. I grew to love Lucie. I just did not want to become her.

Leaning over the top bunk, I started to complain privately to her about my hair and having to wear those ugly clothes. My head still felt sore, and I had a headache from those chemicals. My appearance was a tool I used to help me survive at school. However, I still would find a way. We were now at an age when looking strange created a challenge for me. Mrs. Haney was clipping my wings, but I would find a way to fly.

One day, when I grow up, I kept reminding myself, *I'll wear the clothes I choose and do my hair the way I wanted.*

Inside I was rebelling, but I kept quiet.

I looked longingly at the two nice dresses and one pair of black patent leather shoes in my closet that I was not allowed to wear; they became symbols of a world that I could view through the other side of the gate of my world. One day, that gate would open for me. I had to wait and try to survive until then.

Touching the dresses and secretly trying them on, I would enjoy the pleasure of feeling the material on my body. It was my secret pleasure. There was no mirror in our room to see how they looked on me, but I still enjoyed putting them on when I could.

Mrs. Haney allowed me to wear them to church, and on the rare occasion when Miss Sweet came, I wore the dress and the shoes, and I remember the "oohing and aahing" as those clothes were laid out.

Ironically, that black-and-white dress and patent leather shoes would play a big part later in my life, in a way that Mrs. Haney could not have imagined.

On school days, along with the heavy stockings, I was forced to wear snow leggings well into the warm days of spring. I would wait until I was far enough away from the house and take them off, along with the heavy stockings, devising small ways to overcome the desire to make me ugly. I longed to be a normal young girl. After I took those ugly stockings off, I would skip the rest of the way to school. Small steps to freedom to just be a kid, enjoying a warm spring day and forgetting for a few moments the darkness of the house behind me, loving the feeling of the air on my legs. Embracing the normal high spirts of a twelve-year-old girl. My birthday came and went in the fall. My birthday went by with no notice. I often forgot them myself.

Anticipating my school day and the kids, without those heavy leggings and stockings, I skipped rope, singing songs as we skipped. Sometimes, I shared the songs I learned at the orphanage, and no one flinched at the songs as they were often about my imaginary dad. Jesus was okay to sing about.

I made friends with other students because I enjoyed being around kids from normal homes. They provided a glimpse of life inside the gate.

The family attended a church at the end of the street. Mrs. Haney was a Sunday school teacher, and Mr. Haney was a Sunday school superintendent.

Once a year, they presented a play, and I took part in it. For that occasion, I wore a costume. That year, it was *The Merry Widow Walz*. I imagined myself dancing with a handsome prince dressed in a beautiful Victorian gown. I had a head full of imagination and dreams: a girl waiting for the dance to come. Glad I would take part in the play. The beauty that Mrs. Haney was trying to hide would be an asset in the play, so I was to be used on that one occasion.

On the day of the performance, my ball of perm was covered with a floppy hat, and my large glasses came off. I wore a pretty costume that transformed my appearance. For a few moments, I became a princess. I rarely looked at myself in the mirror, but when I did that day, I was surprised. This was the first time I was aware that I was not ugly at all. It was a welcome surprise.

Back at the orphanage, when we did inspection lines for prospective foster parents, I had learned that being cute helped. I tucked that knowledge away on the day I looked at the person I was becoming in the mirror. My looks and the brain I had been given were both tools for survival. I learned that the person who would make survival happen would be me.

What I did not realize was that those very things that were assets in the world would be liabilities when it came with dealing with Mrs. Haney.

When I grow up, I said to myself in the mirror, as I knew I would once again be covered in those ugly clothes and once again be viewed as an ugly duckling.

At the house, Lucie was starting to relax with me.

We had many conversations at night alone in our bunk beds. She was my coach. I would lean over from the top bunk, and she would sit up in the lower bunk. In that position, we would have quiet whispered conversations. She gave me many warnings, like, "Don't get Mrs. Haney angry, or you will be sorry."

As the days went by, Lucie would give me a weather report on Mrs. Haney's moods.

"Be careful, Mrs. Haney is in a bad mood today."

We developed our own form of sign language and were able to communicate in silence when we needed to. Reading facial expressions became an art between the two of us.

Lucie would sense when these moods happened. I would stay out of Mrs. Haney's way, and I tried to ignore them, but her laughter made me cringe, as it was too loud and hysterical. There was a change happening. A storm was approaching in the house, and everyone was tense. Mr. Haney came and went, a shadowy figure in the background next to her dominating personality. He became quieter too.

At mealtimes, I would keep my chatty self-quiet.

We all instinctively hushed and tiptoed around the house. We were trying to be invisible. When we spoke to each other, we would speak softly and sometimes in whispers. We would stifle our laughter. If we broke out in laughter, suddenly she would appear and break the laughter up.

We became quiet, solemn kids. When her moods were bad, we

learned things about her body which gave us a warning. Mrs. Haney would press her mouth together in a thin line and hum softly to herself; I could feel her suppressed fury.

The atmosphere was ominous. We were missing the dark music to go with it, our own horror movie. However, it was not a movie. We were living in the middle of it.

Several events occurred that led up to the final climax, forcing me to do the thing I was not supposed to do. The explosion did not happen at once, but it was a series of events that culminated in that day. Increasing in intensity and weirdness, the household was on tiptoe and started to retreat to the shadows, trying to hide from impending doom.

"Get into the kitchen," she would tell us.

We would not hesitate because things could get worse in a moment. Lucie gave me her warning look. We would walk quickly to the kitchen. The boys were with us on those occasions. We gathered into the kitchen, facing an unpleasant ritual that became frightening in its ugliness. The four of us remained quiet. This was not a fun time, and we all just wanted to get through it.

This was the weekly washing of the milk jugs used to make skim milk from powder.

We would get in an assembly line, washing and drying those jugs, passing them to each other and handing them back to Mrs. Haney. Standing with her mouth pressed together, she would hold the jugs silently up to the light and find a smudge and hand it back to us. This routine would go on until she finally got tired of it, and we were all able to disperse. Mrs. Haney was a large woman and seemed enormous to me in her power. In those moods, she was a monster in the house. She was not the monster under the bed. She was real.

The inspection of the milk jugs was tedious. I had the urge to throw the jug at her. I discarded that notion quickly, of course. However, I hated that ritual. Everyone was relieved when she stopped, and we would be dismissed, which we did quickly, either in front of the television or in my case with a book.

Endlessly creative in the suffering she could inflict, the milk jug ritual became minimal in the events that lay ahead.

It could be the glass milk jugs or it could be washing the floor on our knees and making us go over that floor, standing over her victim of choice and shouting. Increasingly, I became the victim of choice.

Things began to intensify.

One evening, in the middle of the night, I was in a deep sleep and suddenly woke up with a jolt to feel Mr. Haney's arms around me. Feeling like a dream, as I was not fully awake.

Waking up, half-asleep, he was lifting me up out of bed and carrying me down the stairs. I was waking up to a nightmare that was real. The first time it happened, I screamed out, and he shushed me. I was terrified, as I had no idea what was happening. He was a small man, but I was like a feather in his arms. That feeling was unpleasant as he walked down the stairs carrying a shocked girl.

Downstairs, Mrs. Haney stood in the middle of the room, with her arms bent and her hands at her waist in an accusing, aggressive stance. Mr. Haney plopped me down before her. Sleepy-eyed and barely awake, I fell on the floor and looked up at her from the carpet.

"Where is my diamond ring?" she demanded.

"What ring?"

That question raised her fury. I did not have the foggiest idea of what she was talking about. She repeated the question again. I had no response and tried to make sense of what was happening to me. Her threatening voice and her anger caused me to freeze.

She pointed mutely to Mr. Haney, and he obediently lifted me up and forced me over his knees, whipped up my nightie, and started whacking me with a paddle. No further words were spoken.

"Get back to bed," she ordered me.

Confused and shaken, I did as she said.

Crying and sobbing, I went back upstairs and climbed into my top bunk in the darkness; Lucie put her hand out and briefly clasped my fingers as I went past her to climb into the bunk, totally shaken to the core. Lucie knew what had happened.

Did she go through the same thing? I asked myself.

Waking up in the morning, as I stumbled out of bed, I had a new fear of more of those nights. I gulped down my breakfast and ran to school. Mrs. Haney found her ring in the washing machine a few days later. No apology was made.

Stripping now became part of every punishment. I do not know what was worse, the stripping or the whacks. I think the stripping. I was now entering my thirteenth year, and the changes in my body created in me the natural need for privacy that came with those changes. This was shattered. I was budding into a young woman. Shame became an unwelcome enemy to my soul, nipping at the buds of an emerging flower and threatening to still my growth.

My sleep was interrupted several times by many unjust accusations.

My weight was dropping, and the baggy clothes started to hang more like a tent on my small frame. My appetite was gone. Constantly living in fear and anxiety, food turned to cement in my stomach. I would sit at the dinner table for hours. The same food I could not force down would appear at the next mealtime. This became another form of torture.

The house was now an unsafe place for me. The atmosphere was escalating into violence, and I had no defense against it. Running or speaking to anyone was not an option.

I remembered Miss Sweet's warning about running away:

"If you run away again, you will be sent to the place for juvenile delinquents. You will be locked in a jail for bad girls."

Mrs. Haney had tremendous power to do whatever she wanted to do with me.

Lucie could not be an advocate. She was trying to survive too.

I had been a sunny-natured little girl, and this irritated her. A sense of humor often lightened intense moments and helped me to survive. The ridiculousness of events that had nothing to laugh about I could often find humor in.

However, I learned not to laugh or giggle too much when she was within hearing, adapting a solemn, serious face and remaining quiet when she was around. I was beginning to understand daily how Lucie became Lucie. The days were long. Those days, we seemed to be in waiting. Sometimes, in our bunk beds, I would succeed in making Lucie laugh. Laughing in the face of that amount of darkness brought a fantastic feeling of relief to both of us. This was a mental trick I used, stopping me from tipping over to despair. However, I had to restrain it.

As the household was waiting, like the stillness in the air before thunder and lightning, I wondered what we were waiting for.

Obediently, I trotted every day to school in those ugly clothes, and I made friends. At school, I could be myself. Soon the clothes became a trivial inconvenience. My mind was inquisitive, and at school, my own love of learning came alive. School was a relief.

At home, things grew weird. My sleep was constantly disturbed.

Help me survive, I prayed.

I tried.

Lucie was always quiet, but now, she seemed afraid. Albert's naturally sunny disposition had changed as well.

Albert and I used to joke with each other, but he was scared too, and he did not smile any more. We were all a sad group of kids. We used to laugh at television shows, but during those days, we did not laugh.

Walking under the shadow of Mrs. Haney, we were on edge. We were getting paranoid, feeling she was watching every move we made.

Rick distanced himself as well. He was trying to stay scarce. We were communicating our uneasiness to each other, but the darkness was gathering.

The only laughter that was heard was Mrs. Haney, sometimes late at night, and it was often preceded by one of those midnight spankings. I began to hate that laugh.

Finally, it came, like the wave of a tsunami.

One day, the boys and I were in the dining room after dinner, and we heard strange noises coming from the kitchen, crying and noises of spanking.

"Whack! Whack!"

Arthur giggled nervously, and the older boy, Rick, nudged me and whispered, "Let's go."

He was warning me. He and Arthur ran quickly upstairs.

However, I was too curious; I poked my head around the door and beheld a horrible sight.

Lucie was lying over Mr. Haney's knees, fully exposed, and she was being hit by a wooden paddle. She was moaning and crying. Her exposure took her humiliation to a deeper level. Lucie was closer to a young woman than a young girl, which made her shame even deeper.

I loved Lucie, and my fire started to rise.

Frozen with horror and shock, I stood in the dining room, unable to move.

Mrs. Haney stood with her arms folded across her chest, watching the humiliation of Lucie with a grim look of satisfaction. The boys had thankfully disappeared. At least they did not witness Lucie's humiliation.

What could quiet, shy Lucie have done? I wondered.

I knew she would have been innocent.

Mrs. Haney saw me.

Stomping up to me, she ordered me up to the bathroom, where I was to stay. She gave me a shove, and I made it upstairs.

I sat shivering with fear in the corner of the washroom. Soon I heard the dreaded steps on the stairs. Mrs. Haney stood in the doorway of the washroom with a box of detergent and a strange looking contraption, a rubber bag with tubing.

Now she gave me instructions, performing her penetrating procedure and saying over and over as she did it that I was a dirty, dirty, girl. It was agony. So painful that I screamed. Her roughness and the mantra she kept repeating while she performed the task filled me with shame.

Wounded and full of pain I stumbled back to my bed. I could barely walk.

Lucie sat on her bed, looking shocked; we did not speak, caught up in our own individual fear, two defenseless girls in our own private agony. My screaming brought the police. The neighbors complained. Several years later the incident was noted on the files I was able to obtain. That procedure was not repeated.

The house was quiet as a tomb. What was coming next? We all worried. The other kids knew something I did not know. Things would get worse. *How could they get worse?* I wondered.

Other abuses quieter and more deadly started. Mrs. Haney had the freedom to do whatever she wished, and she had a willing enabler in Mr. Haney.

Rick added his part in the weirdness. He started making unwelcome advances, adding another layer of tension in my life. He disgusted me.

One night, when we were left alone, he chased me around begging me for a kiss, brandishing money.

"Just give me a kiss," he pleaded, "and I will give you a nickel."

Fed up with that, I ran out of the house and hid in the neighbor's back yard, which brought more unwelcome attention to the house. Furiously, Mr. and Mrs. Haney spanked Rick in front of all the family. I felt sorry for him. We were all embarrassed.

The torture became quieter, but the shame and humiliation increased. The punishments became more bizarre. Stripped from the waist down, I would stand facing the wall for hours, while everyone walked around me.

What was my infraction?

I was the infraction.

My spirit was not broken.

Mr. Haney lifted me up on an ironing board and strapped me face down, again stripping me from the waist down, and left me for hours in that state.

"Next time, we will beat you in that position."

There were no limits to this torture. I would limit them by my own resilience. My goal was to stay alive and grow up and leave this house of torture. Miss Sweet's threats remained with me. I could not run. I was powerless. If I ran, I would be in a prison for girls. I was between the devil and the abyss. I was trapped.

Finally, I was driven to jump over the cliff, with the devil at my back.

Chapter 14
THE ESCAPE

School became a place where I slept. My head would fall over a book, as my body was craving sleep. A teacher called someone, as I was showing up at school with gaunt eyes and falling asleep at my desk. Mrs. Haney was furious. No one knew why I was sick, why I was losing weight.

At some point, they thought I had scarlet fever, so the house went into quarantine, and I remained in bed, finally succumbing to sickness. There was a disconnect between the abuse I was going through and the fact that I was getting sick. Eyes turned away.

A psychologist talked to me, and I shared with him what I was going through. He made a report, and years later, I saw it. There was a note of compassion mentioning "bizarre disciplines that should be investigated." He also noted my intelligence and expressed concern about my education. However, nothing was done, and that day, I was unaware of the report.

We were still under scrutiny due to my illness. The house remained under quarantine. We were stuck together in that bleak place. No one could leave for the time being, until they found out what was wrong with me. Lucie and I were separated, as I was moved into Rick's room. We were deprived of our nightly conversations and the comfort we gave each other.

Lying in bed, I was counting the tiles on the ceiling. I was alone in Rick's room, and everyone was downstairs watching television.

The hours of my days dragged by; one day, I crawled out of bed and went to my old room to fetch one of my books and my stuffed animal. Climbing back into my bed with the book in my hand, I heard Mrs. Haney coming up the stairs. My heart started hammering in my ears. I quickly hid the book and my stuffed animal under the bed.

She burst into the room, holding a mop over her head.

"I told you to stay in bed," she said.

Cowering against the wall in my bed, I sat with my back to the wall. She proceeded to beat me with the mop she was wielding.

Finally, thankfully, worn out from her fury, she suddenly left. Feeling that I had come close to death, I slowly rolled over. I picked up my glasses from the floor that had remained intact. When I hid the book, I had hidden my glasses under the bed to hide that I was reading. Full of pain, I managed to stand up. My legs buckled down under me. I steadied myself with my hand on the bed. From somewhere deep inside I summoned the energy to run.

My floppy-eared friend was under the bed, hidden. Grabbing it and a sweater, shoes, and socks, I stood up, laying them on the bed. Slow and deliberate. Trying to restrain panic.

Raising my nightie over my head, cringing with pain and stilling the feelings of panic, I pulled one of the baggy dresses on, carefully and deliberately trying to avoid my wounds. The dress worked well for that, as it fell loosely over me. I carried my shoes and wore slippers to muffle the sounds of my descent. I would discard the slippers when I got far enough away from the house. I knew I would need my shoes for walking. I slipped on my sweater to make it easier for me. The sweater would cover the stains seeping through from my wounds on to the dress. I had always used that sweater to add some shape to those oversized dresses. Planning to look as normal as possible. As I gingerly got dressed, I attempted to control my shaking. Trying to focus on the escape, not the beating.

The brokenness that Mrs. Haney wanted to achieve had broken my body but not my spirit. I sensed she would find out soon that to break my spirit, she needed to kill me.

Fearing for my life, I decided to run.

The television was blaring downstairs. Someone had turned it up to drown the sounds of my screams. This worked well for me in the moment.

Sounds of activity drifted up from the kitchen. I could hear Mrs. Haney, as supper hour was approaching. I was not certain what time it was, but I thought it was close to Mr. Haney coming home from work. I did not have much time. Urgency was pushing me.

Lucie and the boys were watching television, which meant they would not see me at the base of the stairs near the front hall.

I held on to my shoes and my stuffed animal, continuing to fight pain. Panic was rising in me and threatened to overwhelm me, so I struggled for control.

Sheer will and determination overcame that threat. Fearing Mrs. Haney would kill me if she caught me trying to leave.

My feet whispered softly down the stairs. I slipped quietly out of the front door without any incident. Nobody shouted out. I ran down to the sidewalk. I paused briefly at the end of the driveway and saw Mr. Haney's car coming up the street.

Reason was failing me, as I should have known that Mr. Haney would do nothing. He had intervened once when Mrs. Haney left the living room briefly in one of those night encounters.

He had placed his hand between the paddle and my skin to stop the force of the paddle and told me quietly to cry out. He went along with Mrs. Haney. She enjoyed the cruelty.

He was the enabler of it. He did not enjoy it but did not stop it.

He got out of his car and stopped before me, looking at the house, looking for Mrs. Haney.

"She beat me with a mop," I said. Hastily I told him what had happened.

I rolled up my sleeves showing him the evidence.

Frustrated, because I knew that looking for help from him was futile. I was trying to hurry. I kept looking back at the house. I was expecting Mrs. Haney to burst out of the door any moment. Mr. Haney was nervous too, looking worriedly at the house.

He immediately started to defend her and to blame me.

"You shouldn't have left your bed," he said.

He barely glanced at my injuries and kept looking back at the house. I knew with a sinking heart he would not help me. He was too afraid of her himself.

"Stay here," he said. "I will go and talk to her."

He turned and hurried towards the house.

I ran.

Chapter 15

THE RUN

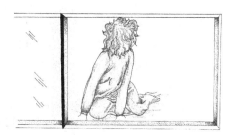

I ran until I was out of breath, and then I kept walking, with no idea where I was going. I kept off the main road but continued to walk in one direction on the side roads. Finally, feeling I had done that long enough, I started walking on Victoria Park, heading into the city. Putting as much space between myself and the woman, I walked and walked.

As shock wore off, my body was starting to scream at me. Sadness filled my heart. The pain in my body was eclipsed by my fear.

There was no going back, and the future was uncertain. I was too young to be on my own. I had no plan. Fueled by desperation, I kept walking.

Emptiness and deep loneliness created its own darkness. I felt danger in that darkness, a soul sickness, cancer of the soul, which could spread and had the power to destroy. It had its own life, and I was fighting it with comforting memories.

Clutching my floppy-eared friend, I was remembering Miss Julie and how she had lifted me up in her arms.

Remembering her singing, "Let the little girl dance, let the little girl dance." Those memories of the orphanage told me that I would find love.

As I walked, I recalled my brother Freddie, who had loved me, and deep inside, I knew I would find love again. My imaginary dad also walked with me on the Toronto streets. Freedom was beckoning to me. Pulling myself out of the threatening depression by remembering the songs I had learned at the orphanage and humming them softly to myself.

The sounds of the city gave me comfort. The honking of cars reminded me of a world that kept on turning. Life was happening around me, relentlessly moving forward, and I did too.

As the day started to approach evening, I grew aware of my surroundings.

I thought of Lucie. She might feel that I had abandoned her.

I knew she would miss me, but I hoped she would understand I had no choice. I had to leave. Thinking of Lucie made me sad, as I knew she would never leave that dark place. Raising my voice might mean she would be rescued. However, no one was listening.

Fall was in the air, and as the sun started to set, the day was becoming cool. Awakening from a trance, I realized I had walked so far that the Toronto streets were busier as I headed deeper into the city.

Trying to be invisible and hide my distress, I passed fellow walkers.

I had no plan. I only knew what I was walking from, not what I was walking to.

A couple of stray puppies came up and sniffed at me. Boy, I could identify with those dogs. *Were they lost too?* I wondered.

I patted their heads; they looked up at me with hungry eyes, and when they found out I was not a source of food, they wandered away. The brief comfort of patting their heads felt good.

Needing to use the washroom, I looked around. I was thirsty and hungry.

A nearby restaurant looked busy enough, so I slipped inside and used their washroom and was thankful for a small water fountain, which helped my thirst. No one took any notice of me. The long dress and the sleeves hid the injuries.

Some of the wounds had bled, and the dress had stuck in places. In the washroom, I wet some towels and went into a private stall to wash myself.

I also made some order of my hair and tried to fluff up my stuffed animal. I whispered to it in soothing words, "We are going to be all right, Sammy. We will find a place to sleep."

I had named the animal Sammy and talked to it. At thirteen years of age, I was just a child fighting a grown-up war. That stuffed animal reminded me of Miss Julie.

I knew it was a minor miracle that I still had it.

Trying to ignore the smell of food, I slipped back out to the street.

I was alive. The relief of that thought alone was starting to hit me.

On that busy street, I worked hard to hide my distress when walkers drew near, I held my head up and looked straight ahead, giving the impression that I knew where I was going, that I was on a mission.

The neighborhood was changing, and the traffic was less busy. The day was descending into darkness. The walkers were thinning out as I was passing a quieter residential area. Soon I was walking alone and peering into the windows of the houses.

Some of them had commercial fronts with their signs offering various business enterprises. They were beautiful old Victorian row houses. Darkness had settled over the city and the street I was on was quiet. No pedestrians, and no cars.

One of the houses was under renovation, and the basement window was open to the street. The upper level looked dark and vacant. The window I was looking into was small, and the floor was covered with construction rubbish.

My weariness was overwhelming. Coldness was starting to seep into me, and my need for sleep was causing me to close my eyes while I walked. I was falling asleep on my feet, with one step in front of the other like a robot, startled awake when my foot would stumble. Pausing, I peered into the window and made a fast decision. This looked like a place where I could rest for a brief respite. My body was demanding sleep. I did not want to stop, but I had no choice. I pushed the window open and climbed through, carefully lowering myself down to the floor, trying not to fall hard. I managed to avoid that, as the window was near the floor.

Clearing some of the rubble, I created a space to lay down. There was no softness to put my head on other than a paint-stained cloth floor cover crumpled in the corner. I managed to create a small pillow for my head.

There was a dim light coming through the window from the streetlight outside. Wearily, I lay down.

Curling up in a ball on the floor, I was soon asleep. In my dreams, I was still walking, as I had walked for so long, it was carried over into my sleep. I do not know how long I slept. It was pitch-dark when something woke me.

Startled awake, I heard a tapping at the window, and I sat up with my heart pounding. The room was dark, but I could make out the white face of someone peering down at me.

"Miss, miss. You'd better get up out of there or the police will arrest you."

His urgency got me up. My body was screaming at me. Due to sleepiness and pain, I moved gingerly over the rubble on the floor and looked up at the white face of a man in the window peering down at me.

"Come with me," he said.

I hesitated, uncertain for a moment, but I was too tired and cold to resist. He appeared kind, and his soft voice filled in the void of loneliness and desperation. My fear of being arrested extinguished my fear of the stranger.

He reached his hand through the window, and grabbing his hand, between the two of us, I managed to climb out in a semi-stupor.

He took my hand gently and led me to the house next door; we went inside and walked up the narrow, dark stairs. The warmth of the house enveloped me.

Emotionally devasted by the cold and hunger, I followed him into a room at the top of the stairs.

A grand piano assumed the bulk of the small room. Against the wall was a sofa and a lamp.

We had made the climb up the stairs silently, and other than his warning, we had not spoken further. He remained a shadow, as the room was dark. He led me over to the sofa and indicated for me to lie down. Mutely, I did, too tired and sleepy to ask anything.

Kindness was all I sensed from him. On the sofa, I lay down and put my head on a pillow. He covered me with a blanket, and I clutched the stuffed animal to me. In that moment, I was simply a tired and physically broken child. The devil could have led me to that sofa, and I would have done what he said. There was no resistance left.

He bent down and whispered something in my ear but did not touch me.

It sounded like, "Sleep now, my child."

Then he left me and sat down at the piano and started to play.

The room was filled with music. Beautiful music. With my untrained ear, I knew it was exceptional.

The man's hands danced across the piano keys, and the heavenly sound carried me into another world. The music became part of my body, swirling around my wounds and my brain with healing power. Along with the music, the room was filled with peace of a sort I had not known since the days of the orphanage. I forgot my hunger. I forgot everything in that moment.

I could see shadows in the room and the darker shadow of the man at the piano, and my eyelids closed on the vision.

I fell asleep.

When I woke up, the early sunlight filled the room. I looked around; the piano sat empty and silent. I was dazed and confused; the previous night felt like a dream.

He was gone. I was not sure what to do. He had felt safe in the night, but in the chilly morning light, I was uncertain. He seemed so nice.

What would he do if he stayed? Would he look after me? Was he safe? What if he wanted to kidnap me?

These questions rolled around in my mind. Rolled around and around, in an endless circle. I was torn. He had given me so much comfort, and my heart longed for that. Fear conflicted with my longing, and fear won.

Sammy, we must go. Men can hurt girls.

I got up as fast as I could manage. My aching body protested. I knew I had to leave the comfort of the room. I needed to run again. I was confused about what had happened, and I was afraid to wait until he came back. Trust slipped away.

Back down the narrow stairs, I left out the front door into the sunlight of the morning. The house I was leaving felt empty. Wondering about the silence of that house added to uneasiness. There was no safety for me. Out on the street, I felt a little safer.

Disheveled and wearing a long-rumpled dress and laced-up shoes, clutching my floppy-eared stuffed animal, I must have created a different picture. I was old enough to be on my own, but well into my thirteenth year, I looked like a child. My hair had not seen a comb, and my dress was stained. The dress was a dark brown, so the stains were barely visible.

However, the morning was cool, and the sun kept slipping behind a cloud. I began to feel cold again. The old enemy, shaking, was starting up, and I was trying to stop that from taking hold. Hunger was gnawing at me.

Again, I started walking and walking aimlessly in the city. With no sense of direction, growing closer and closer to the center. Movie theatres and bars were becoming more frequent. Despite the situation I was in, I felt the excitement and buzz the city gave me.

My stomach was gnawing with hunger and making gurgling noises. This was early afternoon. I was slowing down, looking for a restaurant, although I had no money. My hunger and the need for a washroom was driving everything else out of my mind when a man drew up alongside me.

"Are you lost?"

"No, I am not lost. I am just going for a walk."

"Would you like to go to a movie?"

"Sure."

I was surprised but welcomed the attention. I knew I needed to eat. This would solve the problem of a gnawing belly. He did not look much older than me. Just a boy.

I thought I could manage him. He could be my life jacket. He was an older teen, around sixteen to eighteen years old. He did not look threatening. As disheveled as I was, I was surprised a boy would be interested. Still clutching my floppy-eared friend, Sammy, I looked twelve years old. In my vulnerability, I was no threat to him, either. My hunger took precedence over any other concern.

Food!

Hot dog, French fries, popcorn, coke, and candy went flying through my mind. I was forming a plan. I would get food and run.

"My parents allow me to stay out until it gets dark," I lied.

This was late afternoon, so I thought that would give me a few hours.

Food was uppermost in my mind.

In we went, and he brought me popcorn and a drink, grabbing some candy as well. My favorite: butterscotch candies.

His name was Ray, and we settled down to watch the movie. I chatted away to him. I put my drink beside me in the seat and held on to the popcorn on my lap and bit into the hot dog. I was starving.

In my pocket, I loved the feel of the candies, which I intended to save for that night.

The movie started to play, and for that moment, I was just a girl.

My first bite of the hot dog was in my mouth and the bag of popcorn was on my lap, which I was trying not to spill. Sammy was happy too. For the moment, we were safe.

My eyes widened with a mouth full of my first bite.

Across the bottom of the movie screen, my name was scrolled along with my description and a number to call.

"Five feet, two inches, petite, blonde girl, aged thirteen is missing. If you see this girl, please call this number."

The alert described my brown dress.

That was a huge surprise for me because no one cared about me, and I thought I could disappear. The beating may have frightened Mr. Haney. I could be beaten, but I could not go missing.

"That's me," I exclaimed, pointing out the scrolling notice to Ray. Suddenly, I felt important and could not resist telling the truth. Whispering, I told him what had happened and who I was.

His head swung around in the dark theatre and drew back from me with fear.

"Let's go," he rasped.

He quickly got up from the chair, and we hurried out of the theatre.

Outside the movie theatre, Ray turned to me. I was still eating. My hunger was my priority. I could see he was upset, and I needed to wolf down as much food as I could. I had no idea where my next meal would come from. The reality of that drove out all other concerns.

"You lied to me. You must go back."

Sighing, I gave up. His manner had softened when I showed him the wounds on my arms, and he knew I was telling the truth. He really was just a boy. Lonely too. All I knew is that he had been kind to me.

"You must go back," he repeated.

He convinced me. Off we went to the police station. He left me there and walked away.

I walked into the front doors of the station.

"Hello," I said, "I am June".

Chapter 16

A WORLD WITHOUT PITY

My name did not appear to impress the police officer behind the desk, so I tried a new statement.

"I am lost."

He just sat there looking at me and did not get up.

"I think you are searching for me," I added.

Now he looked at me with some interest and stood up. He was a big man and towered over me, finally seeing me.

"Where do you live?" he asked.

"You can't take me back there," I replied. "I will be hurt again."

That got his attention, and he came towards me. He took in my appearance. In one hand, I had the remains of the popcorn, and my other hand clutched my floppy-eared friend.

"Come with me," he said. We walked into the back room.

A group of men in uniform gathered around me, and someone found out I was the girl who was missing. They called the CAS, which was the number they had. Thinking of Mrs. Haney showing up chilled my heart. I did not trust Miss Sweet, but I was not afraid of her.

The police officer sat me up on a counter and along with my popcorn and candies, I now had doughnuts. I showed them my wounds. They were shocked with my bruises and welts. Their concern and sympathy caused me to break down and cry with relief. Everything was going to be okay. I felt safe.

That is what I thought. I chatted away to them, glad to have listening ears.

Miss Sweet entered through the door shortly after and walked over to me, and once again, I collapsed in her arms. She tolerated this, but her body stiffened. This raised an alarm, as I felt her cold anger, which she did not display openly to the police officers. The stiffened body gave me an unwelcome message. I was afraid and confused.

She disengaged the hug quickly and turned to the police officers. My momentary hope was lost. The comfort I had received from the police officers was gone. I stood there, uncertain. Now I did not want to leave the safety of the police station.

I watched Miss Sweet. The police officers stepped back. Her presence was full of authority. I realized in that moment that they were relieved to place me in her hands. They were not going to question anything, even though I had showed them my wounds.

Miss Sweet set about signing forms for me to be released into her care, and I said goodbye to them.

The police officers thought I was safe, and I knew I was not. I was hoping they would have asked more questions. Would that have changed things? I'll never know.

Some of them gave me a hug, and their fatherly hugs filled my heart with temporary comfort; oh, how I wished I could stay there with them. My momentary respite was ending, and I was steeling myself for what was ahead for me.

I followed Miss Sweet out to her car. She got behind the steering wheel and did not look at me. She beckoned for me to get in the back seat, and the short drive was quiet.

Her manner chilled my heart. Feeling her disapproval coming at me in waves. I remembered her warning.

"If you run away again, you will go to the school for juvenile delinquents. They will lock you up."

Would the beating change things? I wondered. *Surely, once she hears about what happened, she'll see I had no choice but to run.*

Miss Sweet drove us to a nearby restaurant. We sat down, and she ordered our ritual sundaes. My hunger had settled down, but I looked forward to the sundae and the comfort it would give me. The server gave me a second glance when Miss Sweet ordered them. What did she see? Once again, I became aware of my messy appearance.

After ordering the sundaes. Miss Sweet went over to the pay telephones. She had barely spoken to me or looked at me. Her avoidance sent me a message.

This was late afternoon, and the restaurant was empty, other than two women sitting at another table. I sat and waited for Miss Sweet to come back. I watched her talking on the phone.

She appeared agitated, and her words increased in volume. One hand held the receiver, and the other hand was gesturing. I could not make out her words, but it was obvious she was upset. I sat alone at the table with my fear mounting as I watched this. My body was sore, and I wanted to tell her my story, which I had not had the opportunity to share. Her avoidance of me made me wonder what she had heard. She had no eyes for me and therefore no ears.

What did Mrs. Haney tell her? I wondered.

That day, everything was a mystery. Her avoidance of me and her unwillingness to hear my story made me heartsick.

I was hit by a heavy realization. A truth that was hard for me to face. I struggled to assess that with intelligence rather than the raging emotions that threatened to take control. I needed my wits. However, those emotions were overpowering my brain.

Miss Sweet's coldness conveyed to me a reality I did not wish to believe.

My appearance, and Miss Sweet on the phone, was portraying a message of drama. I felt the curious stares of the two women at the other table.

When I glanced over at them, they immediately turned their faces back to each other. No support would be available to me from that source.

All this hit me as I waited for Miss Sweet.

I watched her walk from the phones to the table; her body straightened, and her quick walk back to me spoke determination.

The phone call had decided what stance she must take, and she proceeded. Whatever had happened had given her direction. She had received her marching orders, and like a good soldier, she would obey them. I sensed I had become a problem, and no sign of sympathy was in her manner. Opposite to that was a steely coldness in the look she gave as she made her way back to the table.

I thought about leaving, and I started to look around for an escape. The only escape I could see was walking right past her out to the front door. There was no place to run, and I was not safe. That trapped feeling came back again. There was no sympathy coming from Miss Sweet.

Is she going to take me to that school?

Her small pixie face wore a look of sternness, and I slumped in the chair. She came back to the table, and her words were cold.

"What did you do?"

Putting me successfully on the defensive.

"I got up to get a book."

This sounded weak. Trying to explain the insanity of Mrs. Haney was overwhelming and attempting to do it made me feel tired and defeated before I began.

I sighed to myself. No explanation would appease Miss Sweet and the system she represented. I suspected the phone call had set my fate.

As I looked at her face, I knew I was lost. I would not be believed, as it was all too bizarre. I held my floppy-eared friend closer, trying to take some comfort. The whole conversation seemed hopeless.

"You must have done something else," she stated.

Leaning forward in her chair, she kept her voice low, but her tone was cold and accusing. The look she gave me was one of suspicion and contemptuous unbelief. I felt sad.

Nothing I said would penetrate her.

I began to weep.

"She beat me," I protested. My voice rose higher, and I could hardly talk.

Feeling overwhelmed and discouraged. The two women at the other table kept glancing over. Standing up, I walked around the table to her and started rolling up my sleeves and pulling the dress up to show her my welts and the ugly bruises that were forming. She could not see them, but I showed her enough. I was trying to express my fear and pain to Miss Sweet.

I stood at the table and held my arm out to her; she restrained me with her hand, as she was aware we were drawing attention. The two women at the next table stopped talking and were watching Miss Sweet.

"Sit down," she growled at me in a deep voice.

I immediately sat down with a heaviness in my stomach, which threatened to turn into nausea.

Evidence of a beating was of no interest to her. She had chosen to ignore the evidence. She did not want to see.

Nothing was going to move her, certainly not the inconvenient child who stood pleading before her in that restaurant. The problem—me—had to be solved, and she had formed a plan. Her eyes were on that plan.

This was something I was trying to absorb as our sundaes were placed in front of us. There was nothing I could say or do.

For a moment, Miss Sweet and I were quiet as we started to eat our sundaes. As usual, the sweetness gave me a moment of respite and brief comfort.

As I put the first spoonful in my mouth, my thoughts continued to swirl. Miss Sweet was momentarily distracted. The conversation paused briefly as the realization of my situation became clear. This was an unfathomable world I was in.

The real world was at the police station. That was a world that saw a young girl who was hurt and afraid. The world I lived in had unseeing eyes and stopped-up ears. However, the police station was also unreal. That was a false security that did nothing for me. They had seen, but they had done nothing.

I tried to finish my sundae, hoping its creamy sweetness would do its magic.

The waitress came over to Miss Sweet.

"Is everything okay?"

"Of course," she snapped.

The waitress backed away hurriedly at her tone. She looked over at me with concern. The two women at the other table also looked over with interest. Miss Sweet's response was not reassuring anyone.

As the waitress retreated, the two women got up and made their way to the front door of the restaurant, passing by our table. However, when I looked at them, they turned their heads to the front and walked to the door and left.

Miss Sweet had deftly taken the conversation away from the torture at the Haney's house. Now she wanted to talk about the man and the piano and the young man at the show. She blended the two men into one.

"Where did you sleep last night?" she asked abruptly.

I told her again about the man playing the piano for me.

"He left, and I fell asleep, and he was gone when I woke up."

I attempted to tell her the whole story of the beautiful music, but she ignored it. It was a beautiful story, but somehow, she did not see that.

If I could have left that restaurant and run out the door, I would have.

In that bed, trying to defend myself against Mrs. Haney wielding that mop, I was unable to stop the blows; once again, I was defenseless.

Mrs. Haney had been in a rage, but the cold indifference of Miss Sweet was impenetrable. I was trapped. I pulled Sammy closer and stared at her, trying to absorb what she was implying about a life that I had not experienced.

The piano man had just been kind. It was innocent. What she was suggesting felt creepy to me. She was creating the same feeling I had when I had to stand facing the wall at the Haneys'. I kept wondering to myself why she was twisting everything I told her.

I wished I had not told her about the man with the piano and the young man who had taken me to the movies, but I knew it was too late. She could make up any story. I would not be believed.

As we finished our melting sundaes, she took the conversation in a different direction and started to reveal her plan.

"Just for the weekend. That could not be all that bad. She will be sorry now for what happened."

Stunned, I realized she was suggesting I return to the Haney's for the weekend.

"If you show her you are genuinely sorry, she will forgive you," she said calmly.

I stared at her, unable to respond. The world she lived in was a world of make-believe, where truth got all muddled up and confusing. It was her reality.

Does she want me to go back there? I asked myself in disbelief.

I knew the woman I had run from would not change. In fact, she may be worse. I had finally opened my mouth, and I had run. She would be angry. Did Miss Sweet want me to walk right back into the lion's den and lay down and be a willing victim? I did not understand.

Miss Sweet with her butterscotch sundaes seemed strange to me.

She looked normal with her big brown eyes and pixie face, spooning the remains of the sweet goodness into her mouth with her soothing, convincing voice lulling me into impossible hope. Somehow, the blandness of her expression and the sweet sundae magnified the evil of what she was suggesting.

I weighed my choices. One was the school, and one was Mrs. Haney.

I did not have a choice. The alternatives were too hard. Miss Sweet told me I should try to go back, then I could avoid the school for juvenile delinquents. Faced with such a difficult choice, I gave in. Beaten down, and wanting peace, I agreed to go back, wishing I could disappear from a world that was so dangerous. Everywhere I looked, I saw danger.

As Miss Sweet gathered her change together, I followed her lead as we both went to the phones.

Miss Sweet dialed the Haneys' phone number, and I waited beside her. I knew I was in mortal danger, and it would be only by my own wits that I would survive as I waited for the voice that would chill my heart.

I took the phone. Mrs. Haney answered, and my stomach flipped over.

"I am very sorry for getting out of bed and running away," I said in a trembling voice. I was choking on my words. "May I come back?"

"You have been telling stories," she said and hung up. I let out a big sigh of relief.

For the time being, I was spared. Mrs. Haney's remark confirmed what I had suspected. I connected the dots that led to that terrible beating. That doctor had made a report, and no one had done anything. Someone had to be blamed, and I was the one. Not Mrs. Haney and not Miss Sweet.

I stood there and tried to figure out how I could find a way to escape.

I handed the phone back to Miss Sweet and mutely shook my head no.

I stood there for a moment, with Mrs. Haney's words ringing in my ears:

"You have been telling stories."

Then the sound of the phone in my ear like the sound of a gavel banging down.

With a grim look of resignation, she hung up the phone.

Chapter 17

THE DELINQUENT

"You are now heading for the school."
Miss Sweet made the statement flatly, pronouncing my sentence as she looked away from me. We walked briskly back to our table. The restaurant was quiet.

My sundae had melted; she quickly paid the bill, and we gathered our things together.

She ushered me out.

Lucie's warning about what would happen came back to me. I would face the training school for bad girls, a prison. The nice names did not matter. It was not a school. It was a place that locked up girls: a prison.

Remembering the warnings Lucie told me at night. Whispering up to me from the bottom bunk. Chilling my heart. She, too, had been threatened with the school. Every day, I looked forward to our nightly confidences. Spoken under the quiet of darkness and secrecy, we kept our voices to a whisper.

Lucie warned me, "It is a place they send girls they cannot find a home for. They will call you a delinquent, and no one will want you."

"I have to get away from this place," I said. "Mrs. Haney is going to kill me."

"Don't run, or things will get worse for you."

"Lucie, she is going to murder me. She hates me, and I am scared."

Sometimes, she would cry, and I would cry. I simply could not be Lucie. She simply could not be me.

"Come with me."

"Please don't go."

"They will lock you up and throw away the key."

"Don't run away."

"If you think it is bad here, it will be worse at the school. The girls are tough and mean, and lots of them are criminals. They form gangs, and they beat up smaller and weaker girls like you. You will never survive."

I knew she was scared. I told her she was beautiful, and one day she would marry.

Looking up from the bottom bunk, her face registered unbelief. Determination filled me to convince her of her own beauty. I had seen it many times in her large brown eyes and long lashes. She had a lovely button nose, and her skin was olive. Beauty that was trying to be hidden. When I was able to make her laugh, her brown eyes would come alive. If she dressed in clothes that fit her and had a good haircut, it would bring out her natural beauty that at the end of the day cannot be hidden. It was her beauty. It was the clothes and her body posture that defeated beauty.

"I will never marry. No one will ever want me. I am too slow, and I am too fat."

"You are different," she said. "You are smart and pretty, and you will be able to marry."

Nothing I said to her in those whispered talks convinced her. Her fear of the school and running away was too strong.

Sitting in the back of Miss Sweet's car, those memories came back to me.

The car remained silent. She drove deeper into the city as the day started to head to late afternoon. It was a beautiful fall day, and the sun was shining.

I watched out the window and had no idea where we were going.

The stiff back of Miss Sweet, intent on maneuvering the car through the busy Toronto midday traffic, gave me no reassurance.

I thought about jumping out of the car. Calculating the risk and contemplating it, I knew it would be too dangerous. I did not have a death wish. We were surrounded by other cars and buses and trucks. There was no break in the traffic. The risk was too great. However, I longed to jump out and run like the devil. Imagining somehow winding myself through the traffic? Then what? That is where my imagining stopped.

Miss Sweet pulled the car over to the curb. As we pulled up to the curb, she broke the silence. She turned around to me in the stopped car.

"This is a receiving center for girls in transition," she said.

Transition? I was relieved we were not headed straight to the school. I did not know that there needed to be a court appearance. Everything was held secret from me.

Miss Sweet turned around in the car and gave me another warning.

"You will be transferred to the school in a couple of days, but I need to take you before the judge for him to sign the order to send you there."

"You are facing this, as you are a juvenile delinquent. Truancy and sexual immorality are the reasons that will send you to the school to correct your immoral behavior."

"What is sexual immorality? What is truancy?" I asked.

She went on to explain; she had created a fictional story.

"What? How?"

Her argument sounded convincing. Who would believe me? Under my stained dress, my body was covered with welts and bruises. Would they tell my story? Not realizing that my deliberately disheveled appearance could support her story.

Would the judge listen to me? Miss Sweet, however, with her brown eyes and efficient manner, had power, along with the organization she represented. I could not speak to that kind of power. I knew it that day as I looked at her.

The longer I went without being examined or given clean clothes, the worse my appearance was. This was not going to help me standing before a judge.

Even Sammy, my stuffed animal, was scruffier. We were a wild-looking pair. At this point, I was a kid with messy hair, a stained dress, and large glasses dominating my small face. My eyes were red and swollen from crying. I looked like a feral child. Bruised and beaten, I had no defense.

"Now, don't open your mouth about the beating or any other of the ridiculous stories, or things will go worse for you."

What she did not realize, and I did not, is that a doctor had written a report that would sit in my hands many years later. That day, my story felt like a secret that would never be told because the consequences for opening my mouth would be too severe. Secrecy became a weapon, a powerful weapon. Shame grew in secrecy and obscurity.

"You broke into the basement of a house. Mr. and Mrs. Haney can tell some stories too. There are places worse than the school, and we can send you there."

Resigning myself for the moment, I would have to find my own way to escape.

Miss Sweet went on to explain to me what to expect at the receiving center.

"There are no locks on the doors, and you will be able to come and go. However, while you are waiting to be transferred to the school, if you run away again, you will not go to a lovely place." Miss Sweet brought her head forward with intensity, underlining her words.

"Then you will go to a detention center, which is a jail. You will wait in a cell."

"Is there any chance that I will not go to the school?"

"No," she said firmly. "As soon as we see the judge tomorrow, you will be transferred to the school."

A jolt of cement hit my stomach with a thud. At that moment, I knew that should a door be opened for escape from the school, I would take it. I vividly remember that moment as my world collapsed. At age fourteen, it felt like a death sentence. How can I describe the huge sense of betrayal to know that everything was twisting and turning before me like a snake? As Miss Sweet bent forward to emphasize her words, I thought I saw a snake in her eyes, reaching out to bite me, and fill me with its venom, and paralyze me in its grip. The venom I saw in her eyes that day was real, and nausea rose into my throat with fear.

Her answer made my own way clear. The place we were heading had no locks. What did she think I would do? A trap opened for me, and I fell into it. Was the trap deliberate? I was headed for what amounted to a prison, and I was housed, after receiving that solemn judgment, in a place that would allow me to run.

The receiving center was a two-story building with a screened-in yard with an area of swings.

The long talk Miss Sweet gave me finished, and we got out of the car. I headed into the front door of the center. I had not been examined about my wounds, and I was still clothed in the stained clothes.

Chapter 18

BROKEN WINGS

I had no belongings other than the stuffed animal I was clutching. Miss Sweet handed me over to a pleasant woman inside the receiving center.

The friendly woman walked me up to my room, which was empty. I asked for clean clothes but was just given toiletries, a cotton nightie, and a change of underwear.

"You do not need anything else," she said.

I was to remain in that ugly dress and was not offered a bath. I asked for one, but she responded that I would get one at the school. This puzzled me. I desperately wanted a bath. My appearance before the judge tomorrow would be in the same dress. *Why?*

Next, she told me about the meals and snacks.

"You can go to the kitchen for snacks of toast, milk, and cookies any time you wish. Curfew is at eleven, and there is a yard with swings at the back."

I had the freedom to come and go. This surprised me. I was being handed an open door, like spooning honey to a hungry child. For the moment, I was tired and needed food and rest to regain energy.

As I headed for the kitchen, I had mixed feelings about leaving. The place was lulling me into a feeling of security because it felt like an eternity since that beating. I felt ripped apart inside in so many ways.

I helped myself to a couple of cookies, intending to go outside to the yard. There was an abundance of food. There was a toaster and loaves of bread, butter, and peanut butter and jam.

There were bags of cookies and bowls of apples and grapes. In the fridge was milk and juice. On the counter were paper bags to put the food in. Looking around with the two cookies in my hand, I was surprised. I headed out to the yard.

This was beautiful freedom. The large yard contained a playground with swings. I sat my sore body down gingerly on a swing and started to swing slowly, with my legs dragging on the ground, sighing with relief at my aloneness, not wanting any more conversations.

The fall sun warmed my face. Sitting there, I felt stunned, relieved, and determined I would survive whatever they threw at me.

My thoughts settled down; I looked up at the sky and breathed deeply, calm on that swing in the setting sun. The combination of the food and the sun started lulling me off to sleep. My body was aching and weary, and my eyes started to close.

Outside the fence, I heard movements, and my eyes opened; I looked carefully, alert but wary. A group of thin, ragged-looking men were moving along the other side of the fence. The men seemed familiar with the place. They appeared more miserable than me.

"Do you have any food?" one man asked.

Barely moving, with my feet dragging on the ground, I was not really swinging. His voice called me back from my doze. He looked in rough shape.

He had a splotchy-looking complexion, and when he smiled, I saw black stumps of teeth in his young face. He had stringy, dirty-looking hair and wore tattered clothes.

My heart warmed with sympathy. Hunger and cold were familiar enemies. I got off the swing and walked over to where they were.

Speaking to him softly through the fence, I instructed him to wait while I prepared food from the kitchen. He appeared to break down in his desperate state.

I wondered, *What happened to the boy?*

In my mind, he could have been my brother Freddie. He was around Freddie's age. I went back inside the receiving center and went to the kitchen. No one was around. The place was quiet.

I quickly set about making piles of toast and jam for him. This was new, and the sheer luxury of doing it gave me joy. The freedom to walk into the kitchen and make my own toast felt special. In my life, I could never freely go into a kitchen and take what I wanted. This kitchen was stocked with Oreos and chocolate cookies and fruit.

Fruit in abundance astonished me. No one cared how much I helped myself to.

The last taste of freedom before I am locked up?

I piled cookies and toast into a bag, and I added another bag of apples and some grapes and oranges.

I was delighted to be able to give something to someone who appeared worse off than myself.

Walking outside through the front door, I headed around to where the men were. I made my way to the young boy.

He was excited, and his big eyes were wide with hunger.

Like a hungry little squirrel, he scampered to me. The other men stood back and waited for him to bring the food back to them.

Because he was so young, they already knew he would be the one who would rouse sympathy. They let him take the lead. They were right. My heart swelled with pity. I would have been wary of the older men.

"I will bring more later," I told him before going back inside.

Later that day, I ate my supper at the table alone.

I went upstairs to my room and waited for a while. The sounds of dishes stopped, and silence settled over the center. I found a book to read.

As evening approached, I went downstairs and began to repeat the process of preparing food for the young man outside the fence. Also, a plan was beginning to form in my mind to make my own escape. Although I loved the luxury of the receiving center, I knew it was a temporary freedom and would not last long. The dark cloud of the prison could not be ignored. The place I was in was soothing me into a lull.

I hurriedly piled food for the boy into a bag, and as I had not asked permission, I was concerned someone would stop me. There was no one around again. As I worked on the toast, I continued to think about a plan. The world was waiting, and in that world was a prison for young girls.

The cruelty I had experienced had taught me to be realistic about what I would face there. I simply could not lay down and accept more abuse. The only defense left to me was to run. I could find the piano man, someone to look after me until I was old enough to look after myself. In my mind, I was retracing my steps to go back to that studio and find him. I was weary and tired of the fight for survival. Every option would be hard. At least at the receiving center, I could take some food with me.

As I made the man some food, I was trying to shake myself from lethargy. After what I experienced, I would have loved to climb into the bed upstairs and retreat for a while. I had to pull up the resolve to fight, but my heart was torn. So far, when I fought back, things got worse.

The front door was open, but I doubted it would remain so for long, as the night was approaching. I was also hearing a television in another room, which made me aware I was not alone.

"Hi!"

I jumped guiltily. I did not think anyone was around. It was another girl, close to my age. She was slim and tall and had an exotic look with beautiful olive skin. Her hair was long and halfway down her back. I was struck by her beauty. She exuded confidence.

"This is for the hungry homeless boy outside the fence," I said.

"Let me help you," she offered.

Next to her, I was again made aware of my disheveled, dowdy appearance. We began to share our stories, as both of us knew we were in transition. Her name was Jill.

Wow, we were sisters. I was to meet many sisters with related stories. I was alone, and her story made me realize there were other girls like me.

"I ran away because I was scared," I said, trying to be blunt and brief. Not wanting to encourage questions.

Jill knew about the school. Some of her friends had gone there. Her description intensified my fear.

"It's like a jail. All your freedom is gone, and there are no boys. No dancing, no fun, and the staff are mean. It is in some forsaken place in the middle of nowhere. We do not want to go there."

The school assumed dangerous proportions. Lucie's descriptions, Miss Sweet's warnings, and now Jill filled me with fear.

Jill waved her arms around as she described the school we were facing. Two young girls standing and bagging food for the homeless outside. We had shelter and food, but we were next to homeless. Would I end up looking like the boy outside, who was the same age as my Freddie? I knew I was near to him. Would I soon be begging on the street?

As Jill continued to regale me of stories she heard, I started to feel panic. Similar panic to when I had slipped down those stairs after the beating, running for my life. At fourteen years of age, I still could not support myself, but the people who were supporting me had become my enemy. What would I do?

"There are no boys there," Jill said. That seemed to be the worse for her.

Not me. Being locked up and at the mercy of people I could not trust was my greatest fear.

Jill was also scheduled for a court appearance.

She told me about the infamous isolation cells at the school, where you could be shut in a little cell for days and weeks. Also, the girls were tough and mean. My heart chilled.

"We should go," said Jill. "We will take some food to those men, and then we will bag some food for ourselves and leave."

First, we took the food out to the men at the fence and then went back inside and filled up some bags of food for ourselves.

Once again, I was trying to still my panic. The television was sounding from the other room, but no adult appeared. We tried to be quiet.

We had no plan and no money. Jill had friends and cousins, and we would head for them. The weather was still warm enough in early fall to sleep rough if we needed to. I also had the plan of the piano man in the back of my mind. Would he want to see two girls? I was not sure.

Jill was a year older than me. At age fifteen, she seemed worldly wise and sophisticated.

We had little time; the evening was closing in fast. I ran up to my room and grabbed my floppy-eared friend from my bed.

When Jill saw it, she laughed in a wonderful way about something she understood. There was no scorn. The laughter had affection in it, as if she too had discovered a sister.

We were not too old for stuffed animals on our beds, but few of us carried them around. I was one of the few.

We ran.

Into the arms of predators.

Soon, two men picked us up. They were strangers to me, but Jill knew them. When we were walking, they called out to us, and she encouraged me to get into their car.

"Hi, Jill," they called out from their car. "Do you want a ride?"

Jill grabbed my hand and reassured me that they were okay.

"They are my brother's friends. They can take us to my cousins."

Her brother's friends appeared a few years older than Jill. Closer to men than boys, and I felt a stirring of uneasiness.

We climbed into the back seat of their car. This was not a comfortable solution for me, but I went along with it in my desperation. Jill, however, was pleased and was flirtatious to the men, which was increasing my nervousness. Sitting down in the back seat, I smelled cigarettes and alcohol. This contributed to my rising concern. Their interest was in Jill. I just came with the package. The glee they were showing reminded me of the pimply boy who had chased me all over the house at the Haneys'.

The car pulled back into traffic and carried us along.

I did not fear Rick because I sensed weakness. These men were different, and I felt alarm that they were strong and jubilant. They glanced at each other with looks of excitement. All my senses were alerted.

It was all wrong, and I knew we were unsafe. Jill was too focused on her flirting and enjoying their attention to sense my alarm and caution. My stomach was clenched in fear.

The driver turned the car off the main road. The paved side road deteriorated into a narrow bumpy road into a ravine. There were trees on either side of the road. Night was closing in, and the road was descending into darkness We were alone on the road. The silence and the increasing darkness surrounded the car.

We were not locked in, as the car did not have locks. I nudged Jill and let her know we were ditching the ride.

I made a secretive gesture, indicating the door. She knew I was serious.

She would either join me, or I would be on my own, and so would she. I thought I had convinced her.

As much fun as she was having, she was clever enough to know this was not a smart idea. I signed one, two, three with my fingers and pointed to the door. She was a good actor, as she kept chatting away to the guys.

So now I did it in earnest. Raising my fingers, I pointed one, two, and three, and we both jumped out into the dark. Jill made a joke when we made our move, so we jumped out in the middle of laughter.

We scrambled up the side of the hill, and the more we ran, the more panicked we felt. My body was still sore, but I ignored the pain.

As we were scrambling, we heard the car screech below. We did not pause and kept pushing harder. We could hear the men shouting in the distance, and it sounded like they were cursing us. We reached the main road.

When we reached the safety of the road, we now bent over laughing out of sheer relief and excitement. The street was busy with traffic and was well lit, so we felt safe.

We did not see the car approaching us. Suddenly, a police car stopped, and an officer walked around the car with his pace close to running. Jill and I both stood still, too scared to resist him.

He escorted us into the back seat of the car. When we told him what had just happened, he told us we were lucky to get out of the situation unscathed.

When we were bent over laughing on the sidewalk, it was my appearance that had alerted the officer right away. My unusual appearance was significant enough to give the both of us away.

Now we would be placed in a secure facility. My new friend had lost her vivaciousness and we sat silent in the back seat. Solemn and afraid.

We felt that the open doors of the receiving center became a trap we both fell into. We took our last chance at freedom. Now we would be locked in a detention center, which was a prison. Our attempt at escape from the school only tightened the case against us. It was a risk we had to take.

The car stopped at a grim building. Grim, as the windows were small and had bars on them. There were several people hanging around outside in groups and smoking. We could see graffiti on the brick walls, and the surrounding neighborhood was commercial. There were no residential houses. We heard a train passing nearby. This was an unpleasant place. There was no attempt to create anything else. No potted plants around or shrubbery. Barren of any of those touches, the place was stark, and I shivered. An ominous chill gripped my heart.

The people we passed appeared rough. One of the men hooted out and said something directed at Jill. A crude comment. We also heard wolf whistles.

We were escorted to the front of the building, where the staff greeted us. Cold efficiency took over.

I followed a woman along a hallway with cells on each side. Jill and I were separated, and I did not see her again. The people I had a glimpse of looked hard and tough. I hoped I would not have to share a cell with one of those women. As we walked by, they called out. Their manner was threatening.

The place was stark.

An eternity had passed, a whole lifetime since the beating with the mop.

Wearing the same clothes and with a body that remained sore from that beating, the beating started to feel like a faded dream. This was only the second day. The beating was secondary to defending myself from other threats.

My body was a myriad of colors. They were unseen wounds until I removed my clothes, and then they became my visible shame. Eyes averted.

A woman in a uniform took me to a small cell and told me to change my clothes. She studiously avoided looking at my bruises. Everyone was, including me. As usual, I started to shake when I changed. She handed me a shapeless gown, a uniform of sorts, worn by the people at the detention center. She put my clothes in a bag, along with my stuffed animal, and took my glasses. I shivered in the light gown. This removal of my glasses and reducing the world around me to a blur happened often. I could not read without them.

Now I was asked strange questions from the woman with the clipboard.

She asked me a barrage of personal questions. I felt invaded and interpreted the questions as accusations. I was embarrassed.

Her questions raised all sorts of worries. In this Alice in Wonderland world, where truth did not matter, I was a kid who felt anything was possible. There were no norms in the world I was living in.

I was baffled about her questions. I was an innocent.

Everything was confusing me. I was questioning myself. Lies that were being formed about me were so convincing, they were almost convincing me. Those lies were relentless. Everything was upside down in that magical world of their creation.

After finishing her questions, the woman left me alone in the cell. That night, I had little sleep. The night sounds were different. Doors opened and clanged shut. Voices shouted out. Guards made their rounds. It was the noises of a prison; there was no happiness there. Chaos surrounded me that night, with the sounds of anger and frustration. It was a strange world I had entered. At fourteen, I had entered the world of a prison. I was there for one night.

In the morning, Miss Sweet arrived to take me to court. After one night in that place, I was ready to raise my hand and plead guilty to anything I was charged with. We needed to go through the formalities that would permit the judge to release me to the school. It was a mock trial, as I had a gag placed over my mouth and had no defense. The juvenile delinquency act required the formality.

I felt dirty. No one had offered me a bath or a comb. I had not been examined by a doctor to investigate my wounds. I still wore the ugly, rumpled, and stained dress that had been given back to me that morning.

Keeping me from a bath or a change of clothes created an image of a dirty girl, which fit the story they created.

I followed Miss Sweet into an official building, and we entered a small courtroom assigned for juveniles. A judge sat at the front behind a desk, and the security bailiff ushered us up before him.

No one represented me. Miss Sweet started talking about a girl I did not know, a girl she had created. She described a girl who liked older men, someone who ran away; she created a fictional story about the piano man and the man at the show, and even included the homeless boy at the receiving center. She did not mention the beating, being locked in a basement, or other abuse. I knew I was done. That's how convincing she was. Over my mouth was an invisible gag. She continuously pointed at me and gestured to me, and I stood there mutely.

The jarring note in her story was me. I stood before the judge, and what did he see? He saw a small girl, still a child, with a long brown dress to her ankles. Short, dirty-blonde, frizzy permed hair. Large glasses swallowed my small face. On my feet were black laced-up shoes, and I clutched a floppy-eared, dirty stuffed animal. I had just turned fourteen but because of my small size, I looked about twelve, hardly a femme-fatale.

I stood there listening to her and was fascinated, astonished by her ability to lie like that. I watched her like I would a traffic accident, drawn to watch and listen, even though the disaster was me.

The judge looked down at me and appeared puzzled; did I see kindness? I felt a flicker of hope.

"She does not look like the girl you are describing," he said. "Is there no one else that would take her in?"

I felt a licker of hope.

Upon the judge's comment, Miss Sweet increased the volume of her voice and continued in a long tirade, taking deep breaths. Then she spoke the two words that sealed my fate.

"She is incorrigible and unmanageable."

Those two words were endowed with great power. I saw the judge's face change, and I heard a sigh of resignation.

Now along with the name "ward," I was an incorrigible and unmanageable ward.

"Alright," said the judge. "She can go to the school."

The papers were signed. Miss Sweet and I headed out the front door of the courthouse.

Chapter 19
BIRDS IN A CAGE

The falcon cannot hear the falconer
Things fall apart
The center cannot hold
The ceremony of innocence is drowned
A gaze blank and pitiless as the sun.

William Butler Yeats, "The Second Coming"

A stormy silence was our companion. Miss Sweet ushered me back into the car and started driving. Neither one of us attempted a conversation. The time for butterscotch sundaes was over. I doubted I would be seeing one of those for a while.

Immediately after the court hearing, we headed straight to the school near Galt. I was relieved I did not have to return to the detention center. I had a bag in the back seat with me that held my books and personal items from the foster home. I was happy to see that the two nice dresses along with my patent leather shoes were in the bag.

There were no stops for butterscotch sundaes or offers of lunch. It was late afternoon, and the fall day still held remnants of sun, with intermittent heavy clouds.

Our drive took us out of the city, and soon we turned off the main highway; the road became quieter, devoid of heavy traffic. My head swirled with the events of a couple of days that had brought me to this car on my way to the school that I dreaded.

The afternoon quickly disappeared into dusk.

Eventually, we turned off a road into the school property, and I was surprised at the expanse of the grounds and the number of brick buildings. One looked like an arena. We pulled up to the largest, which had a Canadian flag flying from a flagpole in front. This building held offices, a large auditorium, classrooms, and a dining room.

Miss Sweet and I got out of the car, and we carried my possessions into the building. There was no sign of life anywhere. It was well past supper hour.

I sat down on the chair pointed out to me in the hall. I slumped down in it and looked around. Miss Sweet stepped away into an office for a couple of minutes and then went out the front door, not looking at me as she exited. As I watched her leave, I knew that would be the last I'd see her. I sat on the chair and waited. I had no idea what to expect.

Soon, a stocky matron with short hair came over and easily lifted my bag, and we walked wordlessly in the cooling fall night. I looked at the shadows as we were walking along. A large shadow and the small shadow falling before us.

My stomach was filled with quivering butterflies. No one was outside.

I looked up at the great expanse of stars and the sliver of the moon.

This gave me a sense of relief and a stirring of comfort because the place had an ominous look to me, seen through the eyes of fear.

I was sensitive to the atmosphere of darkness, as I felt the mood of the place.

Knowing there were girls housed there, the emptiness of where we were walking spoke volumes to me. There was no sign of life. The place was isolated; I felt I had entered a space that was too quiet and removed from the world around me.

This haunting feeling made me shiver, and I realized I would not want to walk alone there at night.

Teenage girls lived there, full of life, but what I was seeing was a place empty of the lives and voices of girls. It was a lovely fall evening, but there was no one out. The voices of the girls had been stilled, and now I was one of those girls.

Starting to think of the girls I was about to meet, I wondered if the rumors were true. Would they be tough? If so, how would I defend myself? I had heard so many stories, and I'd soon find out if they were true. Hence the butterflies. I was apprehensive.

There was a stark contrast between the stillness of the night and the beauty of the stars and moon. I knew there should be life, as 120 girls were housed in those dark buildings, with interior lights showing through the windows, but the area around our walk was very dark.

The nameless woman led me into the front door of one of the shadowy brick buildings.

Young voices came from a nearby room, and I saw girls walking in and out of the room into the hallway where I was. Curiously, they looked like normal kids, intent on wherever they were headed for, and they took little notice of me. They were nothing like I expected. I don't know what I expected, as they had become scary monsters in my mind. They were just girls like me. It was a relief to see signs of life and youth.

Seated around the perimeter were young girls of all shapes and sizes, dressed in similar clothes. Not uniforms, but similar.

They wore blue or grey mid-calf-length skirts and plain

blouses. Bows of green, black, or red were pinned on all their blouses (I later found out their significance). They were pleasant-looking girls between the ages of twelve and sixteen, reading, knitting, and chatting. I was to find out later that they were knitting plain squares that would be joined to make blankets. At the farm I visited, I had watched an elderly lady knit a blanket of beauty. Since that day, I wanted to learn to knit. I was glad to see girls knitting.

Relief flooded me, and I felt my spirit rise. There was a pleasant atmosphere in the room. The sounds of young girls chatting and giggling lifted me.

As I stood beside the woman, they started looking up and noticing me. The room became quiet. My appearance had not changed, and I still stood there, clutching my floppy-eared stuffed animal, creating quite a picture. I knew I looked strange.

The matron clapped her hands.

"This is June. She is a new girl."

The room went silent. Thirty pair of eyes stared at me.

Smirks appeared on their faces. I think the stuffed animal may have had something to do with that.

"Are you a virgin?" Someone yelled.

"What's a virgin?" I asked.

They all started to laugh and my face reddened.

I wanted them to like and accept me; I knew life would be harder if they did not.

I stood, awkward and unsure of what I was supposed to say. Wrapping my arms tighter around myself, I tried to be strong. There were seconds of silence in the room amid nervous giggling.

A young girl took pity on me and stepped forward, shushing the rest of the girls. When she did that, the girls stopped laughing. I could see she was a leader. Now, questions started pummeling me.

"Where are you from?"

"Why are you here?"

"I ran away," I told them simply.

The woman who had brought me in remained silent as this all

played out. The girls started huddling around me. She broke up the huddle and beckoned me to follow her.

The girl who was the leader whispered, "We will see you when you get back from isolation."

Isolation? What was that?

She was letting me know quickly what was coming, but I had no idea what she meant. I was soon to find out. Was she warning me? I sensed this girl would be my lifeline in that place.

The matron escorted me upstairs to the room that would be mine for my stay at the school. Six girls shared the same room.

Discipline at the school created a spartan appearance. Each bed was made up with the sheets pulled tightly over the mattress. No wrinkles on the sheets were allowed. There was nothing soft about the room. This was not a place welcoming comfort.

"We are strict about keeping the room tidy; if you do not, you will get demerit points, and they will effect your privileges."

Matron delivered that message with arms folded across her chest in a posture that reminded me of Mrs. Haney. The room did not invite sitting; we stood by the bed, facing each other.

On the bed assigned to me, there were piles of clothes and toiletries. I was relieved to see a bar of soap and shampoo along with towels. Did that mean I was finally being allowed to bathe? I hoped so. Along with the toiletries were skirts, blouses, and sleepwear. The clothes mirrored what the girls were wearing. An ugly pair of black laced shoes and socks and slippers completed the ensemble. I was surprised that my name was attached to everything.

When did that happen? I wondered. The significance of these prepared items told me that Miss Sweet had notified the school in advance. This was the fourth day after my run, so preparations had been put in motion quickly. The items also told me I was going to be at the school for a while.

"Remove your clothes and put these on," I was instructed.

My name was not used in that brief exchange. No introductions were made, and I did not know her name. No hand of introduction had been offered.

I was feeling the rumblings of hunger, as no food had been offered me. I did not ask, and none was given.

Feeling the grim reality of my situation, dark depression and loneliness were taking hold. This cold, austere place would be my home for an uncertain time. No one had told me how long my stay was going to be. This open-ended situation created uncertainty. Being locked into a stranger's basement, I had wondered if I would be there forever.

That day, I felt the same fear and deep foreboding. Would I be there for the rest of my life? How long would my punishment be? Rights were not given to me to know any of that. There was no end that I knew and no light at the end of the tunnel I was in. I was unable to look up and walk towards that light, creating hopelessness. Not being told was another cruelty.

It was a hidden secret that increased the power over us. None of us were told how long we would be in that semi-prison, isolated from society. This could be a life sentence. I would find this fear hovered over all the girls. It just added to the trauma and kept us cowed and scared and malleable.

The sounds of the girls downstairs drifted up to me, and that lightened me a little. However, I was to be separated from them for something called an "isolation period," which filled me with dread.

Suicide did enter my mind in the middle of my foreboding and fear. In those dark moments, I knew the life I had entered was not a life at all and would hold more dangers for me. In my weariness, my resolve and strength were slipping away. At fourteen years old, I was feeling shell-shocked. When was the next bullet coming?

I stood before the matron and removed my clothes; the shaking started. I reached over to pull the clothes up from my bed. My body had its own voice. Matron looked away quickly as she saw the angry bruises that had turned deep purple.

Was this something she was used to? Girls coming to the school in this condition?

I often wondered that, as I appeared before several adults who seemed determined to ignore my injuries. It took a concerted effort to do that. She did not react to the state I was in. When I handed her my stained clothes, she registered nothing. Instead, she indicated a bag that I was to drop them into.

I was glad to see my dress disappear. I had few clothes with me, but I still had my two precious dresses Mrs. Haney had made and my pair of patent leather shoes.

"We will put those away for you."

That statement gave a little hope. The suggestion was that one day, I would wear them.

I was handed a black bow.

"Pin this bow to your blouse. It must always be worn. All the new girls wear black bows, and as you move along through your time here, you will be given two more bows, each one indicating your time remaining. The green bow means you will leave the school soon. Keeping your room clean and following the rules will determine how soon you will leave and extra privileges."

The privileges amounted to a movie in the main auditorium on a Saturday night, visits to family members, and weekend leaves. I had no family, so that did not matter to me. The length of my stay was all that mattered. I would covet that green bow. I wanted to believe I could shorten my time. After talking to the girls, I learned the actual truth: that promise was just another lie.

"One of the girls will show you the routine when we get back from your isolation period."

I looked forward to that.

The matron escorted me down the stairs and out the building. I looked with longing at the girls we passed by on the way to the front door.

My heart was full of apprehension. Looking up at the matron for her reaction, there had been no connection. She avoided meeting my eyes. What was this isolation? As we passed by the common room, I thought the kind girl looked at me in sympathy. What did she know? What was I facing?

Chapter 20

DO NO HARM

*W*here are we going?
That was the question I wanted to ask, but there was no encouragement for conversation, and I was reluctant to speak up, so I simply followed the woman and did not attempt to speak. Unsure if I wanted the answer.

Instructions were made in sign language, as she made beckoning motions. Her briefing was over, and now I was to simply follow her wherever we went. I had no idea what isolation was. I knew it involved an overnight, as she had placed a nightie and a change of clothing in a bag. Whatever was happening, I would be separated from the girls, which was very disturbing to me.

We entered the darkness of the night and walked around the campus. Once again, I was struck by the silence, which felt like a dark hole of emptiness. Distracting myself from that darkness, I looked up at the beautiful array of stars, which spoke a message of hope and beauty. The moon was still a sliver, but the sky was putting on a show, with stars twinkling at me, counteracting the darkness of the school. They comforted me. It was a cool, crisp fall night, and I forced my body to absorb the beauty, deliberately allowing it to calm my soul. These were the wonderful tools when I could redirect my thoughts,

Something certain in an uncertain world. No confusion there. The moon and the stars represented a certainty.

We stepped up the front steps of a dark building.

"Every new girl is examined before they join the rest of the girls."

Examined? I asked myself. *Are they going to look at my wounds? Finally?*

I did not ask these words audibly. Again, questions were not encouraged. I had no reason to trust the answers. This felt wrong and secretive.

No medical person had examined me. So why now, and why in a dark building away from everyone? All of it felt wrong. The moment of respite, looking at the stars, dissipated.

We walked through the front door; inside the semi-dark building, we went down a hall with doors on either side. The building was silent and empty. The thought of sleeping alone in that empty building added to my sense of something wrong, increasing my feeling of vulnerability. My body resumed trembling. The sound of other girls would have been welcomed. Instead, there was that eerie silence.

We stepped inside a small room, which had a single bed and an adjacent washroom. The woman turned around and stood in front of me.

"Glasses," she said, holding out her hand. These were the first words to break the silence.

Mutely, I took off my glasses and handed them to her. Instantly, my world was blurred.

She reached out for the floppy-eared animal I was still hanging on to.

"You will not need that."

I did not protest.

In taking my floppy-eared friend, she removed the last vestige of my childhood, along with my connection to Miss Julie. My heart stopped for a moment, and I felt a jolt, as if someone had punched me.

I was falling down another rabbit hole that was dark and fathomless. Nothing to grasp to keep myself from falling. Emotionally,

I could feel myself moving back and distancing myself. Like my glasses being removed: everything out of sight, away from me.

I heard her voice from a great distance:

"You will see the doctor in the morning."

She left me. I listened to her steps walking away; they faded away in the empty house, and then the sound of a closing door echoed in the building. Was I alone? The emptiness of the building answered me. My melancholy deepened. I was afraid.

I looked around the windowless space; it looked like a hospital room, with a bed and a pillow with two blankets. I reached into my bag and pulled out the nightgown. Starting to shake, I undressed, put the gown on, and climbed between the sheets. All I wanted to do was sleep, but the night was sleepless.

I wanted to hide; pulling the sheets over me, I tried to restrain the shaking. Missing my floppy-eared friend, I put my arm around the pillow.

Staring at the ceiling, I tried to reach deep and pull something within me to retrieve the sun from the clouds of my mind.

I also tried to escape the feeling that my life, barely begun, was coming to an end in that cold, dark place. Breaking through the despair I was drowning in; I was barely able to breathe. In fact, I was breathing fast and filled with panic as I was facing death. Creating another reality, I tried to slow down my breathing into deep breaths and think.

I loved the sun and just wanted to be free, and so, in my mind, I chased butterflies again with Sarah and got on her red bike and sailed down the hill.

Pulling up the stories of the orphanage into my mind. Miss Julie came to me. Love reached out to me there in the darkness.

I recalled the stories of a man who loved children, a man named Jesus. I had imagined leaping into his arms those years ago, when I was a child of six. Now he remained to me a representative of all that was good. All that was love, as that was the only love I had known.

During the long night, I remembered the songs and prayers I

had been taught in the orphanage and started to raise my voice in that empty building and sing:

—

Jesus loves me this I know
For the Bible tells me so
Little ones to him belong
They are weak but He is strong
Yes, Jesus loves me
Yes, Jesus loves me
Yes, Jesus loves me

The Bible tells me so. (Lyrics by Anna Bartlett Warner)

—

Singing the song lifted the darkness and eased my panic. The sound of my voice broke the dark silence of the night. My voice echoed in the silence. I just sang songs for a while. Finally, I fell asleep with tears running down my face, even in my sleep. In the morning, my pillow was damp.

I woke to the sound of a door opening.

A woman came in, wearing the uniform of a nurse. She handed me a hospital gown and instructed me to put it on. Immediately, the shaking started. I wrapped the flimsy gown around me, as there were no ties. I tried unsuccessfully to connect with the nurse, but she avoided my gaze. She stood there mutely, watching me.

We left the room and walked silently down the hall to another room, where I saw a stretcher and medical instruments. The room was cold, and the lights were dim.

The nurse beckoned me to climb up on a stretcher and remove my gown.

My ankles were restrained and my knees were raised.

I started to shake.

The shaking grew stronger; I had no way to stop it.

All I could do was look at the ceiling.

My hearing intensified, and every sound was loud in my ears. My heartbeats pounded like sonic booms. My face felt fiery red. The nurse shut off the light and left the room. The room was in darkness other than the glow of a light.

Someone came through the door with a light in his hand. The sudden darkness half-blinded and disoriented me.

The man who entered had an unpleasant cologne mixed with sweat. I found myself holding my breath, as I did not want to breathe in the scent. My stomach started to turn. Moving my head away from the sound and scent of the person. He remained in the shadow.

A sudden thrust left me screaming with pain.

I heard a disembodied voice calmly say in a dry voice, with a hint of surprise.

"We have a clean one here."

I had no idea what he meant.

After the examination, the lights came back on. Without saying another word the man left. The nurse was back at my side.

His unpleasant cologne lingered in the room. His words remained with me in their cruel coldness for the rest of my life:

"We have a clean one here."

When I opened my eyes, I was alone with the nurse.

Without a word, the nurse undid my bonds and helped me to sit up. As I sat up, I vomited. She said a foul word, adding to the foulness of the room.

Sobbing and crouching over, the nurse silently led me back to the room where I had spent the night. Clutching the flimsy gown around me with shaky hands, I tried to cover myself. She had to hold onto me, as I was shaking so much and my knees kept buckling under me.

In the middle of pain and filled with shame, no communication was required or desired. I craved privacy in that moment. The nurse gave me towels and said I could have a bath. I just wanted to be alone, and as soon as she left, I gratefully prepared a bath and lowered my battered and wounded body slowly down into the warm water; it soothed me and brought a sense of cleanliness. I let my body go down into the water as deep as I could. I was broken-hearted. I knew that something precious had been ripped from me.

I covered the washcloth with soap and tried to remove any vestige of that man's cologne. Restraining any vigorous rubbing, I kept soaping myself, trying to remove his scent, bringing the bar of soap up to my nose to remember that smell and nothing else.

Shortly after, I dressed in the skirt, blouse, and underwear the woman had put in the bag for me.

I was escorted back to the building that housed the girls.

It was daylight, and the sun was shining. It felt strange that the sun could be shining. Someone somewhere was enjoying and reveling in the sunny day. In the strangest, weirdest way, I found comfort in that. Somehow, the world would keep on turning, and that would be a source of healing for me. The sun would rise, and the moon and stars would keep on shining. I consciously looked for that, the only security in my insecure world. I was able to be thankful for the sun. I turned my face up to it in the walk back to the house and felt its healing touch. Nothing would ever be the same, I knew. My body felt violated, but I did not want that to have power. Allowing the sun to have more, it worked. My trembling stopped before we arrived back at the house.

Hearing the voices of the girls as we opened the door gladdened my heart. They would help me through the years that I was forced to be at that school. We would help each other walk through that night. We could be sisters, sharing a bond of suffering.

I did not share with anyone what had happened. I was filled with too much shame.

Slowly, the routine of the school and the company of the girls did their magic.

Healing started to happen, at least on the surface.

During the day, I pushed away thoughts of that dark encounter, not wanting to go there. But in the night, terrors invaded my sleep, and I would call out, sometimes waking up and not know why I was crying. Then I would remember.

When I was sitting at my desk at school, my memory still had a voice of its own and would not be stilled.

The girl who had rescued me on the first day was named Jan; she became my friend, the bright spot of my days. Unlike me, Jan had a family. I was an introvert. Jan was not. She had a steadiness to her. Life had handed her a tough blow. She too had run from abuse and had ended up at the school.

When girls came from poverty, their chances were greater to end up at the school because their defenses were weak. They became targets for more abuse, as predators roamed in the male-dominated courts of the accusers. The girls would exchange favors. So ironic, as the girls were thrown to predators like lambs to wolves.

Jan, therefore, was another victim. However, she was a steady rock for me and was well liked by the other girls. She was a pretty girl, with short brown hair and brown eyes. She was bright and took to math well in her studies. This would help her to earn a living in the accounting world.

We were sisters in that place. I still did not share with anyone what happened with the shadowy doctor. I was too ashamed. Instead, we focused on our dreams for the future. In that place, she was a good friend.

She had my back, telling me who I should avoid and warning me of pitfalls. She ended up being a lifelong friend.

None of us shared our deep sorrow. Shame and embarrassment kept us silent. We all had our stories. We all shared the feeling that what had happened to us was our own fault. So secrets remained hidden. We did not realize that under the light of truth, their power would be removed. Our instinct was to bury our secrets, but one day, those dead bones of secrets would live.

Silence is the predator's friend.

Chapter 21

GIRLS LIVING UNDER THE SHADOWS

> It is better to walk in the darkness with a
> friend than stay alone in the light.
> —Helen Keller

In the mornings, after we heard the wake-up call from the loudspeaker on the floor, we would hurry through our routine, making certain everything met with the rules. Each bed must be made up with sharp corners and sheets tucked under.

The person who inspected us checked that we had bows pinned to our blouses. Forgetting or losing a bow was an offense and could cost us demerit points. Too many points would cause restrictions.

We had female caretakers who have merged into one in my mind. They all were similar. Stocky and impersonal, never talking to us other than when we were in a group or in trouble. We all merged into one girl for them, and they all merged into one woman. I do not remember their names.

We did not go anywhere on our own. When we walked between

the buildings, we did so in lines of two by two, with a woman at the front of the line and one at the end, taking up the rear.

We walked in those lines, dressed similar, and that was the reason it reminded me of a religious cultlike community. Our uniformity gave me a creepy feeling. I hated it. Individuality was destroyed. The uniqueness of each person was merged into one blended group. This allowed for abuse because we became nonpersons.

We had our meals in the main building, where the kitchen was; the girls gathered there from all the buildings.

The meals were surprisingly good, balanced, and regular. Physical exercise was part of our daily routine. The hand that looked after our physical health was a benign hand. The malignant, secretive hand walked in the shadows and ignored our mental health.

The benign hand did not know what the malignant hand was doing. They were not coordinated with each other. Not ignorance, just a studious unknowing.

Good meals and physical health had hidden benefits. We skated for hours in the winter in the arena. The routine was healthy. This was an asset, as we were not exposed to the pitfalls for teenagers, especially ones with our backgrounds. No drugs, no alcohol, no smoking. The heavy price was the isolation from society. All our choices were taken away. Our normal teenage years would come later. Once we got out of the school, we were ill prepared to live normal lives of any sort.

After breakfast, we gathered in the main auditorium, and a woman with two large dogs walked up the center of the aisle, with one dog on either side of her. I believe they were Dobermans.

It made for a dramatic moment. The woman was slim and tall. It was an imposing picture. She strode up the aisle with the dogs on each side of her, and we all stood up until she arrived at the podium, and then we sat down for morning announcements. The two dogs settled down beside her while she stood and led the morning ritual.

I remember the first time I saw that.

Wow, I thought, impressed.

However, as the days went by. I caught the amusement of the

girls around me. This reduced the impact of this show, and I started looking forward to it. After a while, it lost its power to intimidate, and I simply started to enjoy the morning show.

We all loved that wee bit of drama. This show of power someone thought was needed, her walk to the platform every day, assuming a larger-than-life figure.

Like the Wizard of Oz, she needed props to look powerful, and the Dobermans helped to complete that image. Without her props, she was soft-spoken and seemed shy. Her intimidation disappeared.

During her entrance every day, it became harder and harder for us to suppress our giggles; it would cost us if we got caught, so we managed to stifle them.

Once a week was movie night. We all trooped over to the auditorium in our lines with bags of treats, usually candies. The movies were about teenagers in love.

One of our favorites was the Tammy movies with Sandra Dee. Debbie Reynolds sang "Tammy's in Love," which we all learned the lyrics to. We all wanted to be in love. Boys were not part of our world, but we dreamed of the day when they would be again. I still remember the butterfly kiss a little boy had given me all those years ago.

This was the time of Elvis Presley, and we would swoon over him. My new friend, Jan, was a fan of Johnny Cash and country and western music. Through her, I became familiar with Hank Williams, and I loved his haunting songs of love and betrayal. We practiced dance steps together. Our access to music was limited at the school, and we did not have television.

We grabbed stolen moments sometimes, and we shared our dreams. Any opportunity to giggle and laugh together was precious. We did not share our shame. We could not.

Our hearts were too wounded, and there was a deep fear that should we share our shame, then somehow, we would be shamed again. Speaking about it would make it real, and we wanted to bury it. We wanted it to go away.

"When we get out," became our mantra. We were girls in

waiting. On pause until we got out. Trying to stay out of hot water and survive until then. Our world had stopped for us. Our mental development was frozen in time.

We lived for the future. We wanted to forget the past.

Our school education continued. I enjoyed the classes. We were taught school subjects like a trade school. In school, there was a sense of normal life. We had an English class that was my favorite. Sewing and homemaking were taught, along with hair styling. Secretarial skills were also taught. In those days, it was typing and accounting. The teachers for these classes came from outside the school, and they were refreshing. Their interest in us was kind. They looked at us when they spoke and did not have an angry edge to their voice.

Books available to me were minimal, but my English teacher saw my interest in reading and brought me books to read.

We mowed the grass in rows around the extensive grounds. The campus was comprised of seventy-two acres that needed to be mowed.

We walked in lines, pushing the hand mowers and enjoying that time of chatting between lines as we worked. Those were glorious sunny days.

Mowing in the sun early one Saturday morning, we passed the building that housed the isolation cells. Rumours circled around those cells. Moving closer to each other with our mowers, we chatted.

"Those are the isolation cells."

"That is where you go if you break one of the serious rules."

"Did you hear about the girl that was in there for three months?"

"No, tell me," I said.

"They left her in there too long, and she wrote messages on the wall. She hurt herself to write those messages. No pens or pencils were allowed. An ambulance took her away, and we did not see her again."

The girl leaned towards me, and we stopped mowing as we both looked up in horror at the windows in the building. In the world of school, physical exercise, healthy food, there was always these threats hanging over us. In the middle of a glorious sunny day, that dark building was our own haunted house. I imagined a young girl who had been in there, and I wanted to look away quickly, remembering the long weekend of being locked in a basement. I imagined the cell was worse. I shuddered in the sun.

My encounter with the shadowy doctor took place behind doors, in isolation. There was no open violence, like the secret, quiet abuse Mrs. Haney applied when she was afraid of exposure.

Devising devious means and sometimes more deadly and insidious forms of the same thing.

Like the dogs beside the woman in our opening ceremonies, the threat was always there. The length of our stay, our privileges, and the threat of those cells were shadows over our lives.

In the sunlight of a baseball game, we saw another monster taking place.

Looming before us was another threat. One sunny day, we were enjoying baseball. Looking up from the diamond, we watched the ongoing construction of another bleak building. I felt the ominous darkness of the building. Matron gave us a warning as we looked up inquisitively at the building.

"If you girls do not behave, that is where you will end up."

Feeling a chill at the woman's words, we stood still.

The building was the Churchill House for older girls, and male guards worked there. The isolation cells and that building made the hair on my arms stand on end.

We solemnly listened to the warnings and knew we were being told the truth. Dreadful things could happen.

Girls' lives could be altered forever, like that shadowy doctor altered mine.

We were playing under a dark shadow.

Chapter 22

BETWEEN THE DEVIL AND THE DEEP

Jan and I said a teary goodbye. She was released prior to Christmas. I squirreled away her address and phone number. She was going to Toronto, where I hoped to head to. This softened our parting.

The staff wanted the school to empty out in the Christmas holidays. They were trying to get the girls to contact anyone who would be willing to take them in.

Pressure was placed on me to contact Mrs. James and Mrs. Haney.

Neither of those places would be safe for me. The whole idea was bizarre.

"They do not like me."

"June, I am certain if you write to them, they will welcome you at Christmas."

Do you have any idea what I went through?

It did not appear so, as she kept pushing me to write.

So I gave in and wrote the letter to each foster home to appease her. Certain they would not respond, and I would be safe.

With relief, I got a sarcastic response from Mrs. Haney:

"I suppose you are having fun at school. How is your training to be an airline stewardess coming? Why would you want to come here?"

The comment about my dream of being a flight attendant was a hurtful jab, as that had been my dream. However, I was relieved at her response. I would not be going there.

Her letter, full of sarcasm and meanness, shocked the matron, which confirmed to me that she did not have a clue about what happened to me.

Regretfully, Mrs. James said I could come for Christmas. That woman scared me. I would never go back to her home.

How could I stop this? These matrons didn't know what I had been through.

For me, it felt like suicide to go back there. Mrs. James disliked me intensely. It could have only been out of guilt that she was welcoming me in her home for Christmas. I remembered that terrible weekend she had locked me in a stranger's basement. I could not imagine enduring one of her smothering hugs after what she had done. The thought made me feel claustrophobic. Mrs. James triggered that feeling. No way could I manage that. I forgave her, but I could not be at her mercy. Her moods could change in an instant.

I made my choice. It was not a good one, but it would keep me from going there. I formed an idea in my mind that would close that door. However, it brought risks with it. It was a familiar situation for me, when neither choice was good. Assessing the level of danger, I decided.

Girls were in the habit of cutting initials into their arms and calves. It looked painful and made me squeamish.

The act of cutting, if caught, would take away privileges, and that was my goal.

Squeamish as it made me, I decided to do it in the open, so matron would see.

The other girls used a bobby pin, and I had watched them. It was the only way out of the situation.

I carefully picked the rubber end off a bobby pin, exposing the sharp metal point. Sitting down outside the office on the floor, I openly started picking away on my arm. I sat down on the floor outside the matron's office door, so she could not avoid seeing me.

I kept my head down and focused on what I was doing. Girls were standing back, watching me. Soon I heard the door open and the steps of the matron. She stopped, towering over me. I kept my head down.

"What are you doing?"

I ignored her and continued to work away at my arm, my anxiety increasing at the tone of her voice.

The matron bent down and yanked away my hand that was holding the bobby pin. She did it with such force and anger that the bobby pin fell away on the floor.

"You are cutting your arm," she said.

You forced me, I thought.

"You know what this means?"

I hope so, I thought.

I did not respond audibly because we both knew the results of what I was doing. My privileges would be gone, and I would be removed immediately to the isolation cell. At this point I just wanted her to get on with it.

The matron yanked me up off the floor and made the necessary arrangements to have me taken to the cells.

There was no more talk of Christmas holidays.

Chapter 23
THE CELL

Please give me strength.
We walked in silence.

The weather increased my sense of foreboding, as we walked to the building where the isolation cells were.

That day, when I looked at the sky, the sun had disappeared behind mountains of clouds, reflecting my mood. Reminded again of the Creator, I drew strength from the power that was greater than the woman who walked with me to the cells.

I followed the woman, saying my own private prayer.

I tried to keep my eyes focused on the sky and the reason I was facing what lay ahead for me, as I needed to harden my resolve. Knowing what I was facing was still the better of two choices. I stiffened my back.

We entered the front door, and I was handed over to a large grim-faced woman. She had short, cropped hair like the brush cut I had seen on Elvis Presley. Unfortunately, her expression was like Mrs. Haney's. I often saw that same look and expression at the school. Mrs. Haney was a ghost that continued to haunt me.

Marching upstairs in a quick clip, we kept up the fast pace along a dim corridor. The house around us was silent and dark. The hallway was dimly lit. This added to the atmosphere of the dark building; it had an odor that greeted us the minute we stepped inside. It was unpleasant and hard for me to define.

We came to a door; the woman stopped, pulled out a key, and opened it.

We stepped inside a small room, and she turned and spoke to me for the first time.

"Glasses," she demanded, holding out her hand.

I mutely handed them over. Again.

Handing over my glasses was a warning I was facing something dreadful.

"If you need to use the washroom," the woman said, "knock on the door, and I will come for you."

With that statement, she stepped out of the cell and closed the door in my face.

Turning around, I looked in the dim shadows. The room was devoid of warmth and stank of urine and sweat, with undercurrents of different smells I could not identify: a mixture of unpleasantness.

The misery of previous inhabitants left a lingering residual presence in the room. It permeated the room. It was eerie.

A small bed was placed against the wall, a lone piece of furniture with no mattress, pillow, or blanket. The bed did not hold out an offer of rest. Instead, it looked grim with its barren, cold box springs. If a bed could call out, that one could. It looked stark and lonely. I visualized the girls who had tossed and turned and cried on that bed. I shuddered.

However, again, I stiffened my shoulders.

I gingerly perched on the box springs and tried to find a comfortable spot to sit, but the steel kept moving and pinching my skin, so I gave up.

I stood beside the bed and looked around the cell. The night was fast approaching, and the room was cold. There was no source of artificial light. There was a switch on the wall, but when I flipped it on, nothing happened.

There was a fixture in the ceiling, absent a light bulb. The empty socket stared blankly at me.

Evidence of hands that had deliberately removed any light. The only source of natural light came from a small window too high to look out of. A malignant darkness crept into my bones.

Walking over to the wall, I squinted my eyes and peered closely at scribblings and scratches. I thought I saw the word HELP in shaky letters and thought about the girl who had written messages. Did she leave those marks?

I could feel ghosts in that dark and smelly room.

I was thirsty, with a nervous, dry mouth. Looking around, I could not see a source for water. There was none. No sink in the room or any container of water.

I knocked on the door three times. Soon, the same stony-faced woman opened the door.

She silently stepped back and beckoned me to follow.

Silence felt like part of the punishment. Attempting to make eye contact, I was met with eyes that looked at something over my shoulder. She made the experience as unpleasant as possible.

We walked down the hall to the washroom; I looked at the ugly room and wondered how I could use it. We both stood in that impenetrable silence She said nothing but waited silently.

There was no door on the washroom, no privacy. I tried to control the shaking as I sat down. The bathroom did not look clean. Through all this, everything remained silent, so sounds were magnified, which was embarrassing and contributed to the humiliation.

With arms folded across her chest, the woman remained facing me. She could have been a statue standing before me, cold as stone. Her head slowly turned to one side as I sat down. A small grace, that.

Walking back to my cell, I reminded myself why I had chosen this.

Better this, I thought.

When I got back to the cell, I stood and listened to the sounds. A soft scurrying in the darkness made my skin crawl. I heard a muffled sound of moaning and sobbing coming through the walls of the cell, which created a stab of fear. This was a new sound. *Ghosts?*

Keys jangling and heavy footsteps in the hall sounded outside. I also heard what sounded like someone pacing back and forth.

Lighter steps, a running sound. That kept up for a while with the sobbing, and then silence again. Fear magnified sounds, and when my glasses were removed, this was always the case for me. The room was darkening fast as well, so in the semi-darkness, I was relying more on my hearing and touch.

Curling into a fetal position on the cold floor, I lay with my legs drawn up to my chest, trying to keep the warmth within my body as the cold, dark room threatened to overwhelm me and seep into my soul. Loneliness, deep and fathomless, was filling me up, an all-too-familiar feeling coming at me in waves. I rode against those waves because I knew that was something I needed to fight against. That was the loneliness of isolation.

Unrelenting, this was loneliness that could bring me down into the darkness of insanity. It pushed at me. Anger was a futile emotion, and my emotional energy could not be wasted on that. I fought control. I knew I was in danger of collapsing mentally. I could feel myself slipping. Too much had happened to bring me to that state. I prayed.

I had been told I was to be there for three nights. As the end of the fourth day, I was to be let out. This was the first night I was facing, and I could not imagine any girl being in that cell for one month, let alone three. I had also been warned that should I cry out or make a fuss, my stay would be lengthened.

My creation of my own inner world would get me through the hours.

Three days dragged by. Hour upon slow hour passed slowly by, endless in the boredom and silence. I created stories in my head and dreamed of places I would go one day, imagining a family and a baby I would one day hold, a man who one day would love me.

I said the prayers Miss Julie taught me. Now I lay me down to sleep. I laid down.

I asked Jesus to stay with me and wrap his arms around me, and I believe he did. When I prayed, I was no longer alone.

It was the wrenching loneliness that was the difficulty of isolation.

I counted out the seconds in my head to make the hours go by, trying to calculate in my head and count the hours that passed. The room's changing light gave me an indication. However, much of the day was in semi-darkness. Winter was coming.

Meals were brought to me. In the morning, the mattress was taken away, and a bowl of cereal was brought. Lunch would be a sandwich, and supper would be something tasteless and cold. I was able to judge time by the meals. My mattress was brought back to me after supper.

This was a different kind of abuse, reminding me of the betrayal of Miss Sweet with her butterscotch sundaes, bluntly giving me a death sentence as she spooned the syrupy sweetness into her mouth. This was a beating of my mind and my emotions. I could not run from that. I just had to wait it out. I could not shoo my emotions away like an annoying insect. They were too strong.

My bodily urges shut down, as facing that trip to the washroom was too disgusting and humiliating. I restrained everything and added physical pain because of that. I could not endure that audience of stone.

Thirst was often a problem, as there was no water in the room. My appetite had stilled, along with everything else in my body. Numbness had taken over. Like putting too much weight on a part of the body, circulation was shut down. I needed to do that. I needed to shut down my feelings. I did not calculate that; I was responding with animal instinct.

I fought demons that were rising in me. The devil was in that cell, and I fought him. Daily I fought the devil, and daily I won by sheer determination and the prayers Miss Julie had taught me. The devil could not enter a young, innocent girl with that kind of faith. I would not allow myself to be broken.

My faith had trembling legs, but it was faith nevertheless, and I went through those dark hours with imagination, songs, and prayers, amid dreams. I did not let the demons have their way. When I prayed, the demons slithered away.

We walked back to the home on the evening of day four.

The fresh air hit my face. As I walked beside the woman, I knew I would survive. I once more held the apple in my hand. I was not powerless.

Looking once again at the sky on the walk back, I saw those stars, and the snow was softly falling that night. There was a beautiful full moon.

A song in my soul created peace:

Diamonds in the Sky

On that starry night when the world was still
No darkness could that beauty still.
That night sky was a common grace
Nothing done to me could ever replace.
The moon was full, and in the sky
The angels were singing.
They were the stars.
I had won a battle
Of my mind.
In that starry night
Peace was mine.
My spirit was unbroken, and my mind was clear
On that starry night when the Lord was near.
No darkness could that beauty still
On that starry night when the world was still.
I had won the battle of my mind
In that starry night
Peace was mine.

Chapter 24

THE ROPE

Relief filled me as I walked back into the common room. I stood there and looked at those dear girls' faces, and I wanted to collapse with their arms around me and sob, but I was not that little girl anymore. They looked at me with concern. They knew what I had gone through. Fearing that I would break down in front of them, I rushed to the nearest washroom.

Sitting on the toilet for the first time in three days, I sobbed, wrenching body sobs, allowing myself the luxury of letting go. One of the girls slipped into the washroom, knelt beside me, and wrapped her arms around me, and she sobbed too. We sobbed together. I am certain that girl had her own stuff to sob about.

That night, I was able to sleep, and I could hear the comforting sounds of the girls in their beds beside me, who were snoring and calling out in their sleep, but for the first time, I welcomed every sound. That night, I was glad for those sounds beside me.

The moon and the stars I could see outside the window in my room looked beautiful.

In other places of the world, people were celebrating Christmas. The school emptied out of girls and staff. The remaining girls at the school would go over to the arena. which was set up for skating. We did endless hours of skating around and around the rink. This helped to break up the boredom of those days, while the school classes stopped for the holidays.

Outside the school, the world was covered in snow. We wanted to don a coat and boots and walk in that pristine beauty, but it was not allowed.

There were no open doors to walk through. No one had time to walk with me, and the company would not have been enjoyable with one of those stern women. In those snowy winter days, I longed for my freedom to walk in the crisp day when the sun on the vast fields created blinding light, where sunglasses were needed. Oh, how that world outside those locked doors called to me that Christmas. I knew it would be a balm to my soul. I had to wait, as I could tell a new day was coming. I felt it in my bones. I would be going to a new home soon.

The days were quiet, but I found books to read and learned to knit squares.

After the holidays, it was a relief to return to the routine of our classes.

Miss Bell was my teacher. She saw something in me and tried to encourage me. This was wonderful.

When classes resumed after the holidays, she came over to my desk.

"Can you step outside the classroom with me?" she asked.

We went out to the hallway; I was intrigued and curious.

"June, I've noticed you enjoy reading, and I think it would be nice if you took part in a public speaking contest. The local high schools in the area have a contest every year. This year, I'd like you to enter the contest."

I grinned at her and said, "Wow."

We stood grinning at each other.

"Okay," I said. I was happy to have the chance.

"You must deliver a speech to qualify in front of a panel of judges, and then on the night of the contest, you will give a three-minute impromptu speech.

"You will choose from a choice of three titles. The impromptu speech will be delivered in front of an audience of teachers, parents, and kids at a community hall. The contestants will come from the schools around Galt."

She touched my arm as she continued, in a gesture of encouragement and affection. The last person who had touched me like that was Miss Julie. It was a rare event. In that moment, I was putty in her hands and would have agreed to anything she wanted.

It was daunting to live on a campus that was excluded from society and take part in a contest against kids who lived inside the gate of society.

I started to think about how I would look to them and how different I would appear. This would not be a level playing field.

"Remain calm," Miss Bell said as she watched the expressions of worry cross my face.

Calm? I was a bundle of nerves.

I read my prepared speech to the judges and was accepted to enter the final competition in front of an audience.

My school was aware of what I was doing. This was the first time I had seen interest from the matrons. Arrangements were made for some girls to come to the event.

Attention was turned to my appearance. Miss Bell used her influence and a box that had been put away was pulled out.

In the box were my crepe dress and my patent leather shoes.

I pulled the black crepe dress with raised white polka dots and a white collar out of the box. I tried it on again, and it fit me perfectly. Two years previously, Mrs. Haney could not have imagined the purpose that dress would play in my life.

Rarely worn and then just for show, it was still like new. It had been packed carefully two years ago. The dress was lined with black crepe and had been a little loose, but now it fit me perfectly, allowing for the curves of the young woman I had become. In a classical style appropriate for a speech, the white collar and cuffs finished off the classical look.

What pleasure I felt when I pulled that dress over my head. I had not been allowed to wear it, and finally I was able to. Mrs. Haney's agenda to make me an ugly duckling had not worked. This time, it would be worn for a different show. Next, I tried on the patent leather shoes, and I emerged. The dancing girl would not disappear.

Girls were training to be hairdressers, and one of them carefully shampooed my hair on the day of the contest. She skillfully groomed my hair into softer curls.

Another of the girls handed me a pair of nylon stockings; this was the first time I experienced nylon stockings. They were brand new. She helped me to make certain the lines on the back were straight on my legs.

The stockings were like silk against my skin, and I remembered those dreadful thick leggings Mrs. Haney had forced me to wear. My excitement rose, and I recalled that inspection line at the orphanage when I was six years old, singing and dancing with Miss Julie, "Let the little girl dance, let the little girl dance."

We were all excited, and for once, the staff shared our enthusiasm. This was Miss Bell's doing.

One of the girls contributed light makeup, all lightly applied under the watchful eye of Miss Bell: a little mascara and blush and lipstick. My glasses would be removed for the speech: my choice.

I was treated to a bubble bath, the first in my life. Girls contributed all their treasures, and one of them had bubble bath soap. These were the tough girls I was afraid of? I loved them.

Another girl brought out a mild cologne fit for a young girl and in a scent that was popular among the teens of the day. These preparations were done in the hours before leaving for the community center, where the contest was going to be.

My clothes were laid out on my bed, and everything was gathered early in the day. It was a wonderful time, but my stomach was full of butterflies and what ifs.

"What if I lose?" I asked that question of Miss Bell. "What if I lose?"

"You do not do this thinking like that," she replied.

"If I win, will this help me to be released from the school?"

"I am not sure," she said honestly. "It can't hurt."

The contest was held at a large community center near the school. The other girls from the school along with the matrons settled down into the front rows reserved for them. That night, the school allowed the remaining girls to come who wished to, and a lot of girls came on a bus provided for the occasion. It was a noisy bus, as they were all excited. We loved any excuse for an evening out, where we could view normal life.

The auditorium looked like it had a dual purpose as a gym. The chairs were filling up.

There were three finalists, including myself. In a small room off to the side of the auditorium, a young man held out a basket containing three slips of folded paper. Miss Bell had gone to sit with the school. I was alone with the two contestants and the boy who held the basket for us.

On each slip was the title of a speech. We each chose a title and were to present a three-minute impromptu speech on that topic. We had to take turns, and I was chosen to go last. I looked at my title and was pleased. The title jumped out at me: "The House of Tomorrow."

The other two contestants each took their turn. I did not listen to their speeches. I had the opportunity to share my dream, and I was focusing on my words in my mind.

The hall was filled, with every seat taken and more people standing at the back. Others were standing at the sides against the wall. I could not but wonder if the fact that a girl, an outsider from the training school, was taking part may have piqued their curiosity and therefore the large turnout.

I had looked at the room when the other kids were speaking, and the size of the audience was intimidating.

My turn came.

I walked out onto the platform and stood at the microphone on rubbery legs; my veins were on fire. I kept my glasses off to blur the room. My choice.

My voice sounded clear and distinct. My hands were clenched, and I stood stiff with resolve.

The highlights of that speech remain in my memory because they described a world I had imagined in my mind, in those long slow hours in that isolation cell.

That night, I was given a voice. Nights of loneliness and fear were the catharsis of my speech. The words spoken came from that source.

I spoke of a dream house of tomorrow. I had read about that house a long time ago. Miss Julie had told me that in my father's house, there were mansions, and he had gone ahead to prepare for his children to live in them one day. Out of the words she read to me, I created my dream home. I knew the world I lived in was not the only one. Miss Julie taught me about another place. That place was called heaven. Out of that came my speech.

In my speech, I described a house that was built by God. In that house of tomorrow, a child's voice would be heard. There would be no fear. Love would fill the house.

Miss Julie read from a children's Bible with pictures, introducing me to Jesus, who in my heart became my father. These stories she read to me opened the gate to hope.

Miss Julie told me that in that house, Jesus would wipe away all my tears. Never alone. Never afraid. No one would have to say goodbye. I would feel his arms around me just like in that picture in the front hall of the orphanage. The man who loved children was the only Father I had faith in, not the stuffy unapproachable God I had seen in other churches. In God's house, there would be a huge family. Music would fill the house. Books would line the walls. Miss Julie's words and her faith saved my life. My circumstances in my life became hard, but the reality of the man she talked to me about never fully left my heart. I believed Miss Julie.

I told them that love would fill that house of tomorrow.

That evening, my voice was heard.

My brief speech became a passionate protest. I spent the full three minutes describing that house and expanding on the highlights. I had finally been given a chance to raise my voice, and I used it.

When my voice stopped, the room became silent.

The silence was only a pause. A brief pause, seconds that felt like hours.

There was a rustling of noise. I could see people rising to their feet, and they were applauding as they stood. Not in unison, but I saw them rising throughout the hall, and I stood and waited. The applause rose and pushed me back with its volume because the girls started to shout out, starting with my girls, but they were quickly joined by the rest of the kids.

My face was burning with my emotions of joy and relief at their reaction, and I stood in front of them for a moment or two. I could see Miss Bell and the girls from the school standing there. Their faces were a blur, but I knew she was smiling, and the girls were jumping up and down. Even in the blur of a life without glasses, I could see them jumping and waving their hands.

We were a proud school that evening. My heart knew that this was something special for all of us. I learned that day that I could make my way in a friendlier world. We were outsider kids, but for a moment, we felt the gate had opened a crack.

A memorial of the day was granted to me, a medal with an inscription bearing my name.

Miss Bell wrote a formal letter recommending me for further education. I kept that letter and treasured it for years.

June at age fifteen, on the front steps of Galt Training School for Girls (The Grandview School for Girls)

Chapter 25

RELEASED FROM THE SNARE

> We have escaped like a bird
> Out of the Fowler's snare.
> The snare has been broken
> And we have escaped.
>
> (Psalm 124:7)

For me, life began on my sixteenth birthday. That was the day I was released from the Galt Training School for Girls.

The year was 1959. Elvis Presley had just released "Crying in the Chapel," Frank Sinatra had a hit with "All the Way," and rock and roll was the craze around the world. *American Bandstand* was on television, and the jitterbug and the Twist were popular dances. The Everly Brothers "All I Have to Do Is Dream" came out that year. Crinoline skirts and bobby socks were in fashion for teenagers.

This was the world around me when I was sixteen.

The day before my birthday, the matron approached me after supper.

"You are leaving the school tomorrow," she said, handing me two large plastic bags. "Get your things together in the morning."

I did not sleep well that night, tossing and turning as the night dragged on, waiting for the first light of the morning. When it finally came, I hastily dressed in the school uniform, a heavy calf-length skirt with a plain cotton blouse.

I was quiet as the girls around me were sleeping, but I could not wait. I filled the two bags with my meager possessions, trying to make as little noise as possible. The girls and I had said our teary goodbyes the night before. I would be leaving shortly after breakfast. My heart was pounding, and my hands were sweaty with nervousness, anxious to go, but afraid someone would stop me at the last minute and make up a reason to keep me. Stranger things had happened.

One of the girls had brought me a pair of white saddle shoes she had polished up for me. It was a wonderful gift. She also included a pair of white bobby socks. I did not need to wear the functional laced-up black shoes we wore in the school, which I hated. I stuck them under the bed, figuring I could finally choose my own clothes. That thought set my heart racing with anticipation.

I put the black shoes under the bed, feeling like I was leaving my old life behind along with the shoes.

I did not have any money, but my rent was paid for several weeks. In my purse was the letter from Miss Bell and the medal I had won for the public speaking contest. The letter and the medal were my precious, priceless possessions. Miss Bell had written to the school, stating that I was "above average in intelligence and would be good to provide higher education for June."

Years before, a doctor assessed me and advised the Children's Aid Society that I was a candidate for higher education. Those suggestions were not heeded. Armed with my own wits, I was confident I would get a job.

My skills were limited, and my education was rudimentary. I had just completed grade ten. However, I knew I could learn. I just needed a crack in the door, and I would push it open. I considered nothing else.

Miss Bell and I had not said goodbye. I had left a letter with another girl to give her. The girls were glad for me.

The night before, I had asked the matron, "Am I going to a place where the girls go when they have no family?"

The matron looked at me blankly, and I realized she did not know. Nothing was explained to me. I spent my childhood in confusion. Did anyone know the answers? They did not.

Carrying two large garbage bags filled with my possessions, I climbed into the back seat of the car waiting outside for me. I was the lone passenger out of the school. I was glad of that and looked forward to enjoying the ride, filled with my own thoughts and dreams. The drive to Toronto was silent. An older man and a young girl silent on the trip in our own space. Two strangers in the same vehicle, where there was no connection encouraged or desired. Too many girls with too many stories? Not wanting to be heard. Silence prevailed.

We soon arrived in Toronto, and the car pulled up to a building on Gerrard Street, close to Yonge Street. I was glad to grab my bags and exit the vehicle. I nodded, said thank you to the driver, and stepped to the front door of the building he directed me to.

The building was Willard Hall, which was a woman's residence run by the Christian Temperance Union.

WCTU and the YWCA provided safe places for young women to stay in the city while they were starting their careers or finishing their education. The women were between the ages of sixteen and twenty-five.

I went in the front door and up two steps to another door. One wall of the entrance area was decorated with stained glass. The sun shining through the glass created a first impression of beauty and warmth. I opened the door to the reception area. As I entered, a woman came around the front desk and greeted me warmly.

"You must be June," she said, holding her hand out to me.

When I took her hand, I was filled with relief because her grip was warm.

I was coming in from the cold.

Her name was Miss Bentley. She did not blink an eye when she saw I was only carrying a couple of bags and no suitcase.

After Miss Bentley shook my hand, she took one of my bags and showed me up to my bedroom, where my belongings were placed. There were two beds in an empty room, which was small and functional. There was one dresser between the two beds and a clothes closet.

Longing to explore and imagining walking, unaccompanied, for the first time in two years, I was straining on the leash.

"Could I go for a walk?"

Her first reaction was surprise and then her face registered sympathy. She knew where I had come from.

Understanding, she responded kindly, "Just take thirty minutes, or you will miss your supper. Also, I want to take you around and introduce you to your roommate."

I promised her I would not be long.

I hurried to experience my first taste of freedom.

Running down the stairs, I could not go fast enough, skipping two steps at a time, leaping down them like the kid I was. Opening the front door, the city hit me, with its noise and smells. Cars honking and the smells of the food vendors. A cacophony of sounds and smells. Exhaust fumes, and yet the inviting smell of food and street preachers shouting out their warning messages and the faint music of the street performers. The sound of the horns of a Salvation Army band outside one of the bars around the corner. Drifting in the air was the smell of cigarette smoke. Life once again came alive in me, adding to my excitement, as I loved Toronto. It was the city of my birth. I was home.

The late afternoon was muggy, and a soft rain started. It was an unusually warm day for fall, and the rain felt like a Scottish mist. I ran out the door in good health, with all the energy and vitality of a young girl. No bruises or welts on me that day.

People were hurrying along on their missions. Everything was at high speed, and I loved it. A huge contrast from the deadly quiet, cultlike environment of the school. Girls in long lines of two, in long skirts. Lines weaving around the campus. Never alone, walking from building to building in imposed silence, escorted by grim-looking women.

Now I saw life.

I felt like dancing.

"Let the little girl dance, let the little girl dance." I was a little six-year-old again at the orphanage with Miss Julie. She would have loved to see me with the spirit of the dance filling me.

Welcoming the soft mist that fell on me, I sang, "Happy birthday to me, happy birthday to me," as I walked on those Toronto streets that day. I did not care if anyone heard me or looked at me with curiosity.

I hurried back to the residence, mindful of Miss Bentley's request to return before supper.

She was waiting for me behind the reception desk.

"Okay, June, let's see if we can do this before supper," she said cheerfully.

We started the tour of the residence.

As we walked along the hall, Miss Bentley and I passed girls who looked quite different from the girls at the school. These were privileged girls and comfortable with their lives. Surprisingly sweet and welcoming, taking no pause of any difference in me, smiling and nodding as we walked by. I could see Miss Bentley was well liked.

The upper two floors were similar; they housed the bedrooms and washrooms.

"There are two phones on each floor. You can answer a call, but if you need to make a call, you can go down to reception and have that added to your bill."

I could hear a girl calling out names for other girls. It added to the noise of the place. Something simple like having access to a phone was exciting to me. I imagined I would make loads of friends. Soon they would be calling out my name.

We continued down the hall and stopped at a large washroom. She pointed to the claw-footed tubs.

"You can have a bath as often as you like, but you must take turns with the other girls."

Looking at the tubs, I pictured myself sitting in a bubble bath. At the school, it was jump in and jump out, as there was always a lineup for baths.

This was a luxury, and I added bubble bath to the shopping list I was forming in my mind. I was already shopping with money I did not have. I would be applying for a job immediately.

As we continued our tour, I was feeling optimistic, but there was an undercurrent of anxiety. I had just come out of the shadows. The sun was coming out from where it had been hiding.

We proceeded up the narrow stairs to the laundry room, which had a door to the roof. Miss Bentley did not join me, but I stepped out on the roof, delighted. Walking over to the edge, I took in the view. The area was private and had an enticing view of the city. I could not wait to go up there at night and see the lights.

I could picture retreating there with a book. The area was quiet and private. The noise of the city was dimmed.

I joined Miss Bentley, and we headed down two flights of stairs to the basement; I was pleased to discover they had an indoor swimming pool, which was open early in the morning to late evening. The basement also included a large gym, and I saw girls doing exercises. One girl was practicing dance steps.

We headed back up the stairs to the main level and entered the large cafeteria. The smell of the food grew stronger, and I realized I was hungry.

Miss Bentley had planned the tour well, as we ended up where my roommate was eating her supper.

She showed me where girls were helping themselves to hot and cold food.

"There are three meals a day," my tour guide said; she told me the hours and said that if something caused me to miss a meal, I could go begging in the kitchen.

She laughed when she said that, and my heart warmed.

Miss Bentley also explained the rules of the house. Curfew was eleven on weeknights and twelve thirty on weekends. I was surprised at the freedom.

There were instructions and rules, but none of them seemed too harsh; they were normal rules about order and noise, respecting each other in the residence.

We walked over to a pretty girl sitting at one of the tables who was eating her supper.

"This is Robyn," she said. "She is a student at the National Ballet of Canada."

I suddenly felt every inch an outsider.

Does she know where I have come from?

Chapter 26

BIRD IN FLIGHT

Fighting my nervousness, I went and helped myself to food. I was surprised by the amount of food, both hot and cold dishes and desserts.

I loaded up my tray and joined Robyn at the table. Robyn was lovely. Looking at her, I was planning on the kind of clothes I hoped to purchase, adding more items to my mental shopping list.

Robyn would prove to be one of the nicest young women in the residence. She was popular, and I was fortunate to become her friend. She was a young woman of extraordinary talent and discipline.

Soon I would watch her practice in the basement of the residence, and I occasionally watched her rehearse at the school.

Through her, I was introduced to the other girls.

On the weekends, I was lonely and spent days walking and exploring the streets around the residence, reveling in my newfound freedom and taking in the sights and sounds of the city.

The weekdays were not so difficult to fill once I started my new job. I landed the first job I applied for. Within two weeks, I was working, sorting mail at Canadian Westinghouse.

Robyn pointed out discount stores for clothes as we walked together around the residence.

"I go to second-hand shops," she said. "I get a lot of my clothes there."

This astonished me.

I was encouraged because I knew it would take time for me to have cash to purchase new clothes, and I needed to replace the outdated clothes in my closet.

"When you are ready to shop," she said, "we can go together, and I will help you."

So Robyn and I went shopping for clothes, which was another first for me. We went to the discount stores and second-hand shops she had told me about. We hopped from store to store, and I soon had bags of clothes.

Standing in front of a full-length mirror in my bedroom, I saw a different teenage girl. Gone were the oversized glasses that had dominated my face. I often walked around in a blurry world, as I hated wearing glasses.

I wore a full plaid skirt with a soft blouse. Underneath was a fluffy crinoline, and I was pleased with the softness of it against my skin. I swirled in front of the mirror, loving the way the skirt moved. I was a dancing girl.

The transformation was complete, and now I looked like any teenage girl of the late fifties. I whispered to myself in surprise, "You're pretty."

Years ago, when I was six, someone said those words to me at the orphanage.

No one had said that to me since.

I looked around the room, feeling myself blush.

Along with the shopping, Robyn and I took a tour of Yonge Street.

Lindy's Restaurant was around the corner and was one of the late-night haunts for the girls.

We went there for the freedom and the music.

Pooling our cash, we would play the songs on the jukebox. There was a large jukebox but also mini ones on each table. At that time, I had one song I played over and over called "Endless Sleep."

It was a dark song about a young woman taking her own life. Haunting in the melody, this was in a family of death songs that was strangely popular at the time. I did not know that darkness dogged my soul and could be stirred up. My attraction to that music was an early indicator of that.

The old Comet Theatre was also close by. *Singing in the Rain* was playing with Gene Kelly and Debbie Reynolds. It had been years since I was in a movie theatre.

"We will go and see that," Robyn told me.

I would have to squirrel the limited cash I had been given. My shopping list kept getting longer. Bubble bath soap, makeup, clothes, and now a movie ticket.

Robyn saw my expression and said quickly, "My treat. My welcome gift."

"Wow," I said, wanting to jump up and down.

As we continued our walk that day, we passed several taverns with their doors open. Smoke and music spilled out of the sidewalk, adding to the flavor and scents of the city.

Ronnie Hawkins and his band was an attraction at the Coq d'Or. The atmosphere hit me when I peered inside. Later, Robyn and I along with more of the girls would sneak in the back door and dance together in the darkness.

The management would ignore us. A group of pretty girls was not bad for business. Sailors from the harbor would ask us to dance in the back of the tavern.

Although our backgrounds were different, I was making friends with the other young women at the residence. We were intrigued with each other. Willard Hall did not house orphans.

I was an abnormality. The young women who lived there were from privilege.

They had never met an orphan, and I willingly regaled them with stories. I wanted to make friends. I did not share everything with them. I did not share my shame.

I gave them bits and pieces and kept my secrets safe with Robyn. I was unlike anyone they imagined an orphan would be like. Through Robyn, I now had a circle of friends.

Loneliness was an unwelcome companion on the weekends, when the residence emptied, as the girls often went home to their families.

I walked and walked well into the night; evening was falling into night on one of those Saturday nights as I walked down Yonge to the harbor. It was a long walk.

Sounds of traffic was quieter there, and lights were dimmer. Shadows were falling, and it was dark. The buildings I was passing had emptied out for the weekend.

The lights of the harbor were looming closer. Not realizing the danger I was in, loneliness made me reckless.

I heard footsteps behind me and was startled when a man came from behind and started walking beside me in the increasing darkness.

"Where are you going?" he asked.

"I was just going for a walk."

"This is not a safe place for you."

I saw with relief that he was a police officer. The tall man walked along with me. I looked up at him, impressed with his height. Safety walked beside me.

"Do your parents know where you are?"

"I have no parents."

He looked at me with unbelief. He had spoken to me as he would to a child. His face turned to sadness and concern.

Used to people thinking I was younger, I said proudly, "I am sixteen. I live at Willard Hall."

"Do they know you are down here?"

"They don't care," I said, puzzled by his concern.

"I am taking you back," he said firmly.

Back we went, chatting animatedly all the way, as I was happy to have company, someone breaking up my lonely night. That young man heard my story. I talked about my brother Freddie and how I missed him. As I talked to him, my loneliness faded.

He in turn explained to me the dangers of walking alone at night, especially the area of the harbor, and cautioned me as a father would to his daughter.

"Promise you will not do this again."

I promised.

We arrived back at the hall. Our journey had passed by quickly. The long walk down turned to a short walk back, with company and chatting. I was sorry to see it end.

He accompanied me into the hall and had a quiet conversation with the lady at the front desk. We said good night. I would not make that lonely walk again.

Another night, when Robyn and I were sitting in our beds reading with our pillows propped behind us, there was a knock on our bedroom door.

When I opened the door, Miss Bentley was standing there, and she looked stern.

"June, can I please have a word?"

"Is there something wrong?"

Robyn looked up from the book she was reading.

"Peggy reported that you have stolen a watch from her," Miss Bentley said firmly, "and therefore I need to search your room."

This filled my heart with fear, and the unfairness of it started the trembling. Peggy was a girl who was jealous of my friendship with Robyn. I had never been in her room.

Being accused of stealing could send me back into a dark hole, and I would end up in that ominous building I had watched looming up before us as we played on the baseball diamond. The girls played baseball under the shadow of that building. We had been warned that should we misbehave; we would end up there.

The ground under my feet shook.

The familiar dark feeling of shame was triggered in me; as I stood back and watched Miss Bentley searching my things, I was reduced to nothing, stripped down.

Everything I was trying to make of my life was in danger. I was once again the kid no one wanted. I was not a thief. I knew that if I were sent to that school and ended up in that haunted house, I would not survive. The Churchill House would kill me. I had reason to be afraid.

Robyn had gotten up from her bed and silently slipped out the door. I barely noticed her leaving. She had seen my fear and knew why. I had told her about the school and the building that was being built.

After she slipped out, she gathered her friends together, and they went to Peggy's room. They surrounded her in her room. Whatever they did, Peggy found her watch and retracted her story.

I needed a safe place.

Chapter 27
A SAFE PLACE

> In Mercy's guise I knew
> The Savior long abused
> Who often sought my heart
> And wept when I refused
> Oh what a blest return
> For all my years of sin
> I stood outside the gate
> And Jesus let me in.
>
> —Josephine Pollard

"Hi, my name is John. Would you like to dance?"
"Sure!"

When he asked me to dance, there was confidence in the question. He knew I would say yes. I stood beside Robyn in my new clothes. I could tell he liked me. His eyes were full of interest. There was instant chemistry between us in that moment. His obvious admiration was exciting.

We were in the Red Barn, a dance hall near Oshawa, Ontario. It was a popular place for dancing in 1959.

Standing inside the dance hall, I looked around in awe. Glad

Robyn and other girls were with me. The noise of the place was thundering in my ears.

Sounds of excited young people, mixed up with the loud music. The place was full, barely enough room to fit everyone in. Claustrophobic for me. I felt a glimmering of panic as I realized that moving out of our circle would be difficult, as we were all hemmed in. With Robyn beside me, my panic subsided. She was cool with it all.

Young people from around Oshawa and Toronto piled into their cars on the weekends and headed to the Red Barn dance hall. Celebrities often performed there and drew crowds.

It was a go-to place for kids, the newest hot spot. The dance hall at one time brought in entertainers from Nashville. Johnny Cash, Minnie Pearl, and Marty Robbins were among the stars who performed.

I was prepared to dance. Robyn had helped me to learn the current dances. We had practiced at the hall in the weeks before.

It was wonderful to swing around to the music, in my new skirt with the full crinoline underneath. It was fun to try those novel dance steps. Robyn was an excellent teacher and a wonderful partner. She and I both laughed at my awkwardness. My elegant friend was tolerant. We turned up the music in the gym.

Boys were starting to appear in all our lives. Other girls were dating someone or looking for someone to date. We were all hoping we'd have a dance partner.

We arrived at the Red Barn, hoping for that.

There was special lighting that swirled around the room, adding to the ambiance and dancing on the walls and ceiling to the music. The lights danced too. They looked like stars to me.

The grand music of the fifties resounded around us. Elvis Presley and the Everly Brothers as well as country and western music.

The haunting music, telling tales of love and loss, gave us a chance to slow dance. With the lights turned down, the swooning couples made the atmosphere in the hall electric.

John and I enjoyed dancing that night. Soon he was coming

to Toronto every weekend, and my lonely days were over. I found myself walking around the hall and delivering mail at Canadian Westinghouse, humming the words to "Tammy's in Love." I was Tammy, and I had found my love. "Does my lover feel what I feel when he comes near? My heart beats so joyfully, you'd think that he could hear."

John was the greatest thing that could happen to me. With no family on those lonely weekends, I needed someone to watch over me. John became that person. Not only was he handsome, but he was also a stable, industrious man. Coming into my life at such a time saved my life. I needed protection.

Our backgrounds were vastly different. John was an only child, very loved. He was not dealing with demons. His childhood had given him a good foundation. My emotions rode on an emotional roller coaster of difficulties. He was a steady hand. He did not smoke. He did not drink or use drugs. He was a journeyman electrician, which was physical work. He was in the peak of healthy masculinity. He was my young girl's dream. He fell in love with me, and his love surrounded me. He pursued me and courted me throughout the weeks.

If there was a checklist for a perfect man for me at this phase in my life, he would have met all the requirements. I had no sense at sixteen to fully realize my fortune, as alone in Toronto and still in recovery from the trauma of my childhood, I was more vulnerable than I knew. Certainly, I could have been subject to meeting a different sort of man.

I only knew that John made me feel safe and happy. No more lonely weekends.

My world became John. Robyn was struggling with that, as I was not as available to her. My life became full of phone calls in the evenings, and I sensed Robyn was missing our long talks, as even weeknights were full of my new relationship. John would often come midweek as well as weekends. I was changing. We were still friends, but there was a difference. My focus had shifted, and there was a bit of sadness there, as our relationship changed. She was not as happy for me as I wanted her to be. Instead, I sensed disapproval, like a mother hen to her child. This saddened me, and I did not know what to do about that. I loved Robyn.

John assumed a different place for me.

We would go for exciting rides on his motorcycle. John put his foot heavy on the peddle and skillfully drove us around the winding highways and country roads outside of Toronto.

One day, I was behind him on his bike on the way to meet his parents.in Oshawa, where John lived. We had been talking about marriage.

It was a scorching summer day; after we arrived at John's home in Oshawa, I got off the bike and wandered ahead of John down the driveway to the back yard. John had to do something with the bike and told me to go ahead. It was informal, but he said his parents were expecting me. The formality of the first meeting with John's parents was lost on me. I was ignorant of that entirely. Everything was another new adventure, and I ran ahead to it.

Walking around to the back of the house, the first thing that struck me were the gardens. Standing on the grass and facing the yard, I entered a magical place.

The scent of sun-opened flowers created a euphoric sensation when I breathed in the mixture of scents in delight. Gardens were a new experience for me and had not been a part of my world. I was surprised by joy, stunned by the beauty before me.

Working in the back garden, with a pair of shears in his hands and trimming a shrub, was a man I assumed was John's father. He had his back to me, focused on his work, and was unaware of me standing back and looking at him.

I walked over to him with boldness. There was no hesitation in me. Wanting to say hello, I was anticipating meeting him, certain he would be happy to meet me, considering nothing else.

"I'm your son's girlfriend," I said with pride.

He straightened up and assessed me with a look of disapproval.

What would he have seen? A young girl looking like fourteen rather than my sixteen years. Shoulder-length dirty-blonde hair, full of curls and frizzy on that scorching summer day. Shorts and a T-shirt, petite, with my weight resting at 100 pounds at five foot, three inches tall. My face was bare of makeup. Still wearing glasses that were too large for my face.

"My son has many girlfriends."

He was tall and striking looking, with a full head of wavy silver hair. He turned, after the brief exchange, and left me standing, uncertain how to respond. He continued trimming the shrub he was working on with his back to me.

I was dismissed.

What was wrong? Were my shorts too short? Was my T-shirt too tight? His look of disapproval made me wonder all those things.

Deflated, I turned to the house with the brief exchange still ringing in my ears. I walked into the back door. Sensitive to any hint of rejection, I was wary.

Standing inside the door, I hesitated and tried to prepare myself to meet John's mother.

John had asked me to go ahead into the house, as he was busy with his bike. Now I was not sure that was the right idea. I wondered if I should wait for him but decided to go ahead.

As I stepped into the kitchen from the back entrance area, I was greeted by the enticing smell of cooking food. The mixture of scents of the gardens and the food was creating a wonderful symphony of smells.

The house I stepped into embraced me with its warmth.

There was a woman working at the sink in the kitchen. She turned towards me when she heard me enter the room.

We examined each other. This time, I waited for her to speak. The encounter outside with her husband had taught me to do that. I was going to take my cue from her. I waited.

The woman was plain in the style of ages long past. Out of time. She was in her mid-forties.

She wore no makeup, and there was no effort made to enhance her natural beauty. She was a beautiful woman. Her face was in shadow. The afternoon sun created light behind her. Her eyes were brown and full of expression and depth of character. If purity could be displayed, that is what I saw. Although she wore nothing to enhance her beauty, she needed nothing. The beauty I saw before me was in her presence and her being, rather than her dress.

I stood before her, a waif of a girl on her doorstep.

We connected instantly. She made me think of Miss Julie, her simple goodness, which had its own exceptional beauty, an adornment that covered her.

Her clothes were modest and spotless, with an apron tied around her waist. She was wearing a cotton dress that was crisp and wrinkle-free and covered with miniature pastel flowers. This was a dress she had sewn herself. It made its own fashion statement of a femininity of an era long ago.

I was too old to hug her, but I wanted to. I felt like that hungry child at the orphanage; before me was a woman who reminded me of the only mother I remembered. Unbidden and startling, those feelings were aroused in me.

The atmosphere of the home was powerful and enveloped me with peace. The house was quiet, with the curtains moving at the open window with the sounds of birds. Even the curtains rustling could be heard in the silence. As we looked at each other in those few seconds, the world stilled.

It felt like a healing. The cleanliness and the added touches were simple and effective. African violets that were sitting on a stand in the sunlight, full of their violet flowers.

Two pies were cooling on the table, and something was cooking in the oven, emitting a delicious odor. This overruled my cool welcome from her husband.

I was smitten.

Spending weekends with John's family created safety in my life. The light and the warmth drew me in. I knew it was connected to the God of the orphanage. John's father, seeing that my relationship with his son was serious, warmed up to me.

John's mother was not concerned about my background. She did not know much, but she knew I did not have a family, meeting me with an open heart, although I was dating her son. Her welcome to me was a mother to a daughter. Later, I was to find out that she had always wanted a daughter.

One day, she opened a drawer and showed me baby clothes lovingly kept for years in memory of a baby girl she had hoped to adopt, but things had fallen through at the last moment. In the most ironic of ways, I became that daughter. She had a hole in her heart created by the loss, and I was the girl who came into her life. In my heart was a hole as well.

For a while, I went back and forth to the hall, and every weekend, I would go back to Toronto with bags of food. Huge sandwiches made from roast beef that had been cooked on the Sunday. Fruit and cookies and slices of her wonderful pie. She was feeding a stray that had arrived on her doorstep, too thin.

Every weekend, she made biscuits. The hall had tasty food but could not compete with her cooking. The food she sent back would last me for days.

I soon moved to Oshawa and rented a room briefly near John's home, and within a year after meeting him, we were married.

At seventeen years of age, the Children's Aid Society relinquished control over my life.

I entered the world of marriage and babies. However, there were unanswered questions.

It took decades of recovery until I was finally well enough to seek answers about my family, especially what happened to Freddie. Where was he? Why? That was the big question.

Simply, why?

Chapter 28

LOOKING FOR ANSWERS

"Why wasn't I told?"

Joan, the woman who faced me, looked increasing uncomfortable. She kept shuffling papers around on her desk. She represented the Children's Aid Society.

Sitting with my husband beside me, we watched her shuffling papers around nervously. This was 1998. I had waited a long time and was hoping it was not too long. I was on a quest to find out about my family, especially Freddie.

Joan would not have been involved all those years ago when Freddie disappeared. A fog of mystery covered him. Trying to break through that fog would not be easy.

Looking into my case would have been disturbing. The CAS was her employer.

The nervous moving around of the papers and folders and her posture spoke to me of her discomfort. She had revealed that my brother had written a letter asking about me years before. I had not been told. I was stunned with that information. Hence the question.

"Why was I not told?"

Repeating the same question, as the answers I was getting

back were vague and confusing. Frustration was gripping me at the incoherent answers. Once again, I was entering into that old Alice in Wonderland world, where nothing made sense.

Feelings surfaced, never completely buried, confusion and loss. I walked through the maze of secrecy, looking for missing pieces of the puzzle of my family. I was once again in that Alice in Wonderland world, slipping through the mirror image of my childhood, a looking glass world.

The office created a sense of calm; Joan was pleasant, very courteous, and professional, but her body language and her nervous shuffling of the files in front of her sent another message: a woman who wished she could be somewhere else. She may have been surprised at the real person rather than the child she had read about in her file. That stick figure was not the living, breathing child who had experienced so much trauma. The horror of my story would not have been hidden, revealed in those files on her desk. It would take a steel resolve for her not to be affected, and I sensed she was a kind woman in her nature.

Descriptions in the files were coated in distance and cruelty, making the victim the author of her own abuse, distancing the reader from the child. Compassion did not enter the records. Instead, it created a problem to be resolved, and the problem, unfortunately, was the child. That child was me, an inconvenient child. I had seen those files. They were hard to read.

The humanity of the child was lost under such terms as "case" and "client."

Getting at the truth would be difficult. The truth was hidden in the shadows.

Joan now had the real child in front of her. She started to respond.

"Your experience was not good, and we have evidence in your file that supports your story." That was quite an admission, and I was surprised to hear her admit it.

"I am sorry you went through such a grim time. However, we cannot open your brother's file to you. I can tell you little else."

This was another cautious admission alluding to my "grim time" and that my story was "credible."

She was being careful, and I was making every effort to ease her defensiveness by not taking an aggressive stance. Being aggressive was not going to achieve my goal. Breaking walls of secrecy was my purpose.

I tried to apply skill in my probing: "Yes, dreadful things happened, but I am not on a mission of vengeance. I just want to find my brother."

I leaned forward in my chair and found that despite my desire, my posture was aggressive. I caught myself and sat back.

"Your brother wrote us a letter when he was eighteen years old, asking us about you. He wanted to contact you. The CAS did not think it was wise."

"Please let me see the letter," I begged, stunned at the news.

Again, I sat up stiff in my chair, trying to hide my agitation. She had casually dropped a verbal bomb in front of me.

She had said that Freddie had written a letter and wanted to see me, and they had refused him and had not even let me know.

When he wrote that letter, I was sixteen years old. I was not informed. My heart was filled with the horror of that. My face was burning.

Joan had the grace to look embarrassed. She would not have been involved in that decision. The CAS had the law on their side. They could do whatever they wished, but why? She was forced to defend the indefensible. Keeping my brother and me separated had no justification. The other piece of information was a quote from the letter:

"He wanted to know what went wrong in his life."

Oh, how that broke my heart, and penning these words once again, I feel the pain of those words. Regurgitated in my memory, still the pain remains. I may have helped him, and they did not give me a chance. I dreaded to think what he had gone through.

I wondered if he even was still alive. Although this woman

quoted from the letter, she would not let me see it. This was another cruelty. She told me just enough to break my heart.

On her desk were two files. She had rested her hand on them both. One was open on her desk, and one remained closed. It sickened me to know that one of those files was my brother's file. I desperately wanted to see what was in the file, to see a picture of my brother. I had not been allowed that. I wanted to see the letter my brother had written as a lost boy, another victim to a system I could not understand. With anguish in my heart, I knew he had suffered too. Although years had passed, my heart would always contain love for my Freddie. With a sinking heart, I wondered if I had tried earlier, whether I could have helped him from his own sorrow.

But the steel walls around my brother and the walls of privacy shut me out, impenetrable, and impossible for me to break through.

I would have to find him myself. So much time had passed; I was afraid it was too late.

As Joan saw the expression on my face, her hand closed protectively over the file. I could feel anger rising in me and wondered what would happen if I leapt across that desk, pulled the file from under her hand, and ran with it.

Under the desk, my husband put his restraining hand on my clenched fist in my lap. Joan mumbled incoherent words about privacy.

"We do not know where your brother is. When we learned you were coming, we tried to contact him, but we were unsuccessful. Sometimes, he goes by your biological father's name."

I felt myself slumping back in my chair with defeat. I had to move on.

Then I sat back up with a start when I heard, "You have other siblings: a half-sister and another brother. They have given their permission to contact them."

No Freddie, but two other siblings. I wish I could say I was excited, but the dead-end street to Freddie was making me wary and suspicious of the motives behind this surprising news.

Why them and why not Freddie?

Joan told me about two other siblings I knew nothing about. My half-sister and I shared the same mother but had different fathers. The other was a brother. There was thought he may be a full brother. Why wasn't I told before? Didn't they know everyone would want to know their family? I had no answers to that. I had not even viewed a picture of my mother and knew little of my father. Both of my parents were dead at the date of the interview. I did not know these siblings.

"We contacted them before you came, and they would like to see you."

The system remained unfathomable to me. Who decided what would be told and when?

It seemed sinister.

"Yes, I would like to meet them," I told her.

The first person we met was my brother Robert. He liked to be called Bob.

We went to his apartment in Toronto. As we approached the area and pulled into the visitor's parking lot, we saw garbage littered around the building. The cars in the parking lot were rusty and old.

I was tense and had no idea what this was going to be like. I had not met any member of my family.

We had hugged each other before we embarked. Expectations were lowered when we saw where Bob lived and viewed the people hanging around outside the building. That inner shaking was making itself known, and I was trying to still the unease I was feeling.

We entered a seedy lobby and rang his apartment.

The building had a smell that my husband called the smell of humanity, which was a mixture of sweat, cigarettes, old alcohol, and dirt. The smell triggered memories, and I felt a darkness of depression dogging my spirit.

Bob buzzed us up, and we took the elevator to his floor.

The person who opened the door was a shell of a man, ravaged by time and the terrible things he had done to himself and what had been afflicted on him. He had a thick head of hair and was bone thin.

"Hello, June," he said.

A soft-spoken voice. I knew he was my brother when I heard that voice coming out of that man. Something so familiar, it could not be denied. In the recesses of my mind, I had heard that voice before. Something stirred, a deep recognition.

Did he have the same voice of my long-forgotten dad?

How could I know that voice? I was a toddler when my father died.

However, the voice brought forth a buried memory. Through the shell of a man was a hint of the father we shared.

I shook his proffered hand. We gave each other a perfunctory hug, but I was cautious, disappointed at the shape he was in. The smell coming from the apartment and from the man in front of me was strongly unpleasant.

I tried not to breathe it in and struggled to hide this from him, instinctively holding my breath and afraid I would start gagging. The anxiety and the smell were causing my stomach to heave.

The reality of his life stood before me, and my heart was filled with sorrow at the sight of him. Clarity hit my mind. He was not Freddie, but I was meant to meet him. In that moment, I knew we shared the same mother and father, and we also shared our pain.

He looked the typical homeless man I saw going through the garbage in the city. He did not stand straight but had a bowed posture. His head had the telltale slight nod of a man who had used drugs heavily. It reminded me of those miniature toys called bobble-head dolls.

At one time, he may have been handsome, but he was ravaged from whatever life had given him that marred handsomeness. However, it was still there, that hint of the man he had been, the child before the ruthless hands of fate had dealt their blows. Homeless people would look different to me after that.

Bob was one step away from homelessness. My husband later said he did not believe he could be my brother, but I knew he was. He only saw the shell. I saw his soul.

His face was gaunt. His eyes were the color of mine: hazel eyes, changing colors with moods.

I loved him from the beginning.

There was something in him that I connected to. The next two years with him, until the day he died, was a roller coaster of emotions.

So much damage had already occurred when I met him that it could not be repaired. He had a deep sense of humor, and his intelligence was still there, under all that damage. His language was never course. From the moment we met, he respected me.

My husband and I got involved with him. We went to movies together. We bought him clothes. We cleaned his apartment until my fingers had blisters from cleaners. It was a little selfish, as I was trying to get rid of the smell and be comfortable when I visited, trying to stop my skin from crawling.

Whenever Bob rode in our car, the smell remained in our vehicle for days after. Through all the dirt and frustrations, he remained my brother. He hated showers and was afraid of them. I talked him into getting help with that, but he kicked the guy out of his apartment when he came to the door.

He made a joke at the hospital when he was in palliative care. For the first time in his life, he got treated like a prince. I was so happy I participated in getting him there. He discovered he loved the deep baths they lowered him down into.

"June will be so happy that I am finally clean," he said.

His friend told me that, and I cried. So my brother died clean. And when he was dying, he got treated well. My brother had a wonderful personality, and we shared our sense of humor. The staff loved him.

Two years after meeting him, we buried him. Bob had managed to squirrel enough money away to enable us to bury him. He had pride and an indominable spirit, and I was proud of that.

Bob and I shared something else when he passed. I was able to share my faith in Jesus Christ, and he embraced that faith fully. I had not met the brother I was looking for, but I was meant to find him. My faith tells me I will see him again.

My half-sister and I became friends; she had landed better on her feet than Bob. She had her own journey as well. It is her story to tell.

I would have to keep looking for Freddie. In that search still ahead, I would find more surprises.

Chapter 29

STRANGE THINGS INDEED

"Wow!"
My husband was standing at the kitchen counter with his back to me, preparing our morning coffee. We were getting ready for our day, relaxed, as he was going golfing, and I was headed out to the gardens. Happy to be retired, we were in our country retirement home. The morning was calling to us. The birds were at the feeders, which I had just filled up. His clubs were in his car, and we were having coffee before heading out.

My search for Freddie had continued with no success. It was a couple of years after finding Bob, but I had kept trying. The phone book was open before me, looking for his name in the local phone book. Kirkfield, Ontario, was a thirty-minute drive from my home. I had been told that my mother had lived out her final years there. I often scanned the phone book in Toronto, looking for my brother's name, and now I thought I would look and see if maybe he had moved into the area.

The phone book was open before me to a page where I had found the name I was looking for. When I called out, my husband kept grinding the coffee and pouring the water into the coffee maker, barely acknowledging my exclamation. This was not new to him. There had been disappointments before.

Soon the phone was in my hand. It was a decent time to call. Being careful to remember that not everyone started their day as early as I did, wanting to get out to the gardens early before the hot midday sun.

I dialed the number and held the phone to my ear, starting the same way I did when I was in Toronto. A man had answered.

After introducing myself, I proceeded, "Do you know anyone with this name?"

I told him my mother's name.

"That was *my* mother's name," he said.

My heart started pounding in my head, and everything else was fading next to the thumping in my head. The phone started to shake in my hand.

"Are you Fred?" I croaked.

My throat had suddenly become like sandpaper.

"I am Fred."

He was startled too and agreed we should meet. He gave us directions to his home.

John, as usual, calmed me down; he prepared me for another disappointment and tried to keep my expectations low.

A couple of hours later, we drove up to an address in the country near Kirkfield. As we drove, the country around us became isolated. We drove by small towns and turned up a road that was unpaved. To me, it looked a harsh environment. There was nothing welcoming about the country we were entering. No lushness here, a different kind of country, rocky and barren. Houses sprinkled here and there.

We turned off the main road to a narrow unpaved road. Sitting in the car, I tried to restrain my shaking. *After the long search, was it going to be this easy?* I asked myself.

Soon, we reached a small brick bungalow, parked, and went up to the front door. A man opened the door to us.

We looked at each other, and I was confused. This could not be Freddie. He was too young, and yet we shared the same mother, and his name was Fred. He was shocked, and I was confused. Freddie was two years older than me. So once again, I felt like I was falling down a rabbit hole. The man I was meeting baffled me.

He sat down on the couch in the living room and left the introductions to his wife. He was in shock. His wife was bubbly and welcoming and was the opposite of him. Her name was Donna, and she was full of curiosity.

This man was the one of the final sets of children my mother had, and she had named two of the final sets after earlier children. This was causing the confusion. There were two Freds and two Roberts. This Fred shared my mother with me but had a different father.

Fred was not delighted at this news and was embarrassed.

How did he feel about being named after the first Fred? Would I find another June?

The man who sat on the couch bore no resemblance to me. It was hard to believe we were related.

This finding of siblings was not turning out to be such a beautiful story of reunions. Too much time had lapsed, and our lives had taken different turns. It was not the joyful reunions shown on television of long-lost siblings. Our mother had kept secrets. Fred did not know about me.

"This is where your mother lived," Donna told me. "This was her house.

"I have something to show you," she said. "Come with me. We always wondered who those blonde kids were. No one in our family was blonde."

Donna took me over to a table in the dining room, which was adjacent to the living room. My husband sat down beside Fred. He knew Fred was going through his own turmoil. He sat there and struck up a conversation with him.

I went to the table in the dining room, where his wife indicated a chair for me to sit on.

She brought out an old picture album. She opened the album and set it in front of me. In that album, for the first time in my life, I saw a picture of Freddie and myself. We were sitting in the middle of a field, two urchin kids. My heart was torn with so many emotions. The pictures were taken a year before we went into care. Freddie was five, and I was three years old. I could read a story about that picture.

I sat at that table and stared for a long time. The irony struck me that I had indeed found my dear brother, but only an image of him. I knew him right away. Donna did not say a word. The house held its breath and faded.

Looking at a picture of my mother was a shock. She looked as if nails could be bounced off her, grim and tough. No softness there, and not even a hint of a smile. I turned the pages of the album.

It was a very surreal experience to finally see this woman I could not remember. She was holding my brother and me by our wrists, cold and distant.

Had she already let us go in her mind?

"We found these pictures after your mother died," said Donna. "Every morning, without fail, she would boil a big pot of porridge for all of us on a frigid winter morning," Fred called out from the living room, making our mother real. He loved our mother, and I was glad. His voice sounded defensive. It must have been hard to know this side of her.

"Winters were very hard out here."

It was clear that he wanted to share something good about her. He shared with me how difficult their lives had been in the winter in that little house.

Winters would have been brutal in that isolated place. He told me a little about their lives. How our mother and his father would go into town to the bar to drink. The kids would wait in the car. It sounded like alcohol was my mother's best friend that had become her enemy. I remember the smell of beer Freddie and I had tried to drink all those years ago, when we were hungry. I shuddered at the memory, the two-sided face of alcohol. We had not seen the happy face.

His expressed love gave me comfort. In the world of judgment, it was good to hear. Fred was confronted in me with his mother's past, and he wanted me to know she had suffered, to hear the side of her he loved. I was glad he loved our mother.

I needed space, as my emotions were in turmoil.

Looking at the picture of my mother and my brother was triggering. The picture was a flame that lit my heart on fire, igniting my emotions.

I had spent my childhood without a family, and it was strange that all these unknown people were appearing; they were strangers. They had inhabited a different world than me. We had been scattered all over. All those years ago, a bomb had gone off. Tragedy had happened.

I was in crisis, trying to absorb all this added information.

There was poverty in that home. My own mother had lived and died in the place I was standing.

I got up and walked into the kitchen and tried to imagine her living there.

I stood and looked out the window over the kitchen sink, imagining she was once in the same spot I was standing. Staring out the window at the barren fields, the view was depressing.

I visualized her doing dishes and looking out at the same scene, day after day, in the seasons. She had died when she was sixty-eight years old. Donna said that one night, she went to bed and said she was not feeling very well. During the night, she was gone. Too many cigarettes, too much alcohol, and the harshness of her life had taken their toll. She had eight children; Donna told me that one son out of that set had died in an accident. Yes, she had suffered. She never had the joy of meeting my children, her grandchildren. There were layers of sadness in her life.

It was hard to imagine her living there and that while she was alive, I was spending my summers less than an hour away by car. Neither one of us knew the other one was so close. I tried to imagine that the woman standing there at that window was my mother.

All I felt was coldness in my heart as I stood there. I saw no beauty in that environment.

A sense of emptiness and despair filled me. Dredging up the ghost of my mother made me shudder.

The warming of my heart came when I saw the picture of Freddie and myself sitting in the middle of a field. In the recesses of my memory, the picture stirred something deep inside of me. I knew it was my brother. An old black-and-white picture of two kids.

There were other pictures. One was an Aunt June, my mother's sister, who I suppose I was named after.

However, my Freddie was still a mystery. The man sitting in the living room was not him. He had his own story.

My interest had been to find Freddie, and we were all uncomfortable and ashamed about all the confusion.

There were two Freds and two Roberts. I was glad there was not two Junes.

Donna allowed me to take the pictures with me.

"Would you like to see where your mother is buried?" she asked.

"Yes," I said sadly.

We did not prolong the visit. We were all in our own space of discomfort.

On a day where everything could not seem to be stranger, my husband and I drove to Norland, a small town close by, and went to my mother's grave.

Someone had given her a nice gravestone, and I was thankful for that. A person had cared for her.

Tears started when I saw that familiar name. The name on the gravestone bore my own name. My birth name.

The ground I stood on was near the bones of my mother. This shook me to the core of my being. Everyone I found was either dead or sick. So far, this had not been a happy journey.

Bowing my head in front of her grave, I prayed that she found peace somehow. According to my brother, she had lived a harsh life in that country home. The winters were bleak and cold. The fact that she had named two children after the sons she had lost made sense to me.

It told me she had suffered in her heart about that loss. What torment it had caused her in the dark hours of life.

I could have been her but for an army of angels that had appeared in my life. I knew as I stood there that I had been shown grace.

In the middle of my suffering, I had been loved by Miss Julie, who picked me up in her arms and danced with me and introduced me to Jesus Christ, a woman who had loved me like a mother.

Healing happened. I knew when I stood in front of her grave that day that I had in the end been mightily blessed. I had never been abandoned.

There was no judgment in my heart, only a deep sadness for her and a recognition of our common humanity.

What caused the circumstances to be so hard that she could not raise us?

She had told my sister that "June and Freddie are okay."

Of course, we were not.

Then neither was she.

Appendix

Child Welfare Agencies

In 1952, I stood ready to dive into the new swimming pool at the orphanage. A picture was being taken to mark the occasion. I had been chosen to appear in the *Toronto Star* to let the public know about the pool and celebrate its installation.

A few weeks later, Miss Julie from the orphanage proudly showed me the article and my picture. She had cut it out for me to save, and I kept the article for years. Along with my picture, the article said, "A young 'ward' is enjoying the new pool at the orphanage. 'My name is June.'"

I remember being confused as I looked at the picture and questioned Miss Julie. I simply did not understand that I would be identified as a ward.

That day was the first time I knew I was a crown ward.

Since April 30, 2018, crown wards are called "children in extended care," which is an improvement to the old term.

Presently, there are fifty children's aid societies in Ontario. Each agency is run separately, and the societies operate autonomously from each other.

Twelve are indigenous child and well-being agencies. Three are faith-based societies: Two are Roman Catholic, and one is Jewish. The remaining agencies are not connected to a particular faith.

Each society has a director and a board.

Recently, there have been changes to the care of indigenous children due to the horrific discovery of unmarked graves around the schools these children were housed in, torn from their families. The indigenous people are starting to run their own child welfare agencies.

There is also secrecy in the agencies, as privacy rules apply for minors. Court cases are often shrouded in secrecy because of the ages of the children involved. It is often a juggling act to determine which facts should be made public. As a result, the public is unaware of serious cases that affect the lives of these children. Journalists are the ones who dig out the information, with the goal of educating the public.

Obtaining data regarding children in care is challenging. The latest census was done 2011.

Statistics are difficult to obtain, as children move in and out of care; however, the monthly average is estimated to be ninety-three hundred children in the province of Ontario. Half of these children are youths between the age of sixteen and twenty years old, according to CAS statistics.

There is no central system in Canada. The efficiency and the care of these children in the various agencies can be different, dependent of the individuals and workers in each society and location.

Galt Training School for Girls (Grandview School for Girls)

I described my experience in 1958 at the age of fourteen, living in a training school near Galt, Ontario. The school sat on seventy-two acres of land.

There were five buildings. Three buildings housed the girls. There were 120 girls there in my time, between twelve and sixteen years old. One building contained the isolation cells.

The school was renamed the Grandview School for Girls. When I refer to Galt, it is the same school at the same place. Only the name has changed.

Under the Juvenile Delinquency Act, in 1957, a social worker gained permission from a judge to order me to be incarcerated at the school.

Although I did not take place in the class action suit that happened in 1992, I received a benefit because I was at the school when assaults took place.

Following the closure of the school, former residents came forward with allegations of physical, sexual, and psychological abuse by the staff. This abuse did not become officially known until 1991, when two women came forward who were being treated by the same psychologist. The psychologist introduced the women to each other, and they subsequently made appearances on television. The Ontario Provincial Police and the Waterloo Police Services began a joint investigation in Kitchener.

In 1999, a member of Provincial Parliament, Jim Flaherty, apologized on behalf of the government to the survivors of the Grandview/Galt school.

In January 2002, the Honorable Fred Kaufman, C.M., Q.C., D.C.L., released a report that described in detail the settlement that was made and outlined the abuses that were alleged. The following excerpt is taken from the report:

> While some girls committed minor crimes such as shoplifting, many were sent to the school because they had been pronounced "unmanageable" under the Juvenile Delinquency Act for the reasons such as truancy, the use of drugs or alcohol or "sexual immorality." Many of the young women sent to the Grandview School [Galt] had been subjected to physical, sexual, and psychological abuse by family members. Some were orphans and some were from homes too vulnerable to care for them. Several students at the school were abused during their residency there. The most significant period of abuse occurred during the mid-1960s to the 1970s. The school was closed in 1976.

Isolation Cells

The training schools isolated girls in cells. Those isolation cells were used as punishment.

The United Nations published Standard Minimum Rules for the treatment of prisoners, known as Mandela Rules. These guidelines prohibited the use of isolation as a punishment.

The Juvenile Delinquency Act.

I was sent to the school under the Juvenile Delinquency Act, which was passed by the parliament of Canada in 1908 and revised in 1985.

Acknowledgments

I have heard it takes a village to raise a child, and it takes an army to author a book.

This has been a process that had its beginning close to ten years ago, when an idea formed and became a reality. It started with my grandson, Andrew Del Monte. He came to my home and interviewed me for a school assignment.

"Grandma, you should write a book," he said.

That is how it started. Andrew provided invaluable help and looked at many chapters and gave me feedback. Thank you, Andrew Del Monte.

My lovely daughter Sandra Del Monte encouraged me daily over the years, offering me her much appreciated support. When I was called upon to talk, she provided music with her beautiful voice, choosing songs that helped to elevate my presentation.

Thank you, Sandra Del Monte.

My grandson Adam Del Monte is a graphic designer. He designed the cover of this book and provided valuable marketing services. He has been a constant support all along this journey.

My granddaughter Amanda Lagerquist drew the incredible sketches shown throughout this book. Thank you Amanda Lagerquist.

Thank you, Adam Del Monte.

This book is dedicated to my two sons, Ron Lagerquist and Mark Lagerquist, and my daughter, Sandra Del Monte: my forever family. It is also dedicated to my son, Craig Stephen Lagerquist, who was with me for too short a time.

I have many grandchildren I am blessed with

Aaron Del Monte, Andrew Del Monte, Laura Del Monte, Adam Del Monte, Oliver Lagerquist, Anita Lagerquist and Fiona Lagerquist, Joy Lagerquist, Amanda Lagerquist and Keagan Lagerquist. Faith, Grace and Isaiah Lagerquist.

My son-in law Anthony Del Monte (I call him my other son)

My daughter-in-law, Stephanie (I call her my other daughter)

Brian Henry of Quick Brown Fox has been with me in this from the beginning. His critique classes around the Toronto area assisted me throughout the process.

Thank you, Brian Henry.

Thank you, fellow authors.

Paul Elliott is a worship pastor and a writer, creating several plays in the London, Ontario, area. His prayers and spiritual advice have been a source of help and guidance throughout the process.

Thank you, Paul Elliott.

Delilah Losch is a dear friend who supported me from the beginning. Her support and prayers were constant and never failing. In the early days she would listen patiently as I read aloud portions of the first draft.

Thank you, Delilah Losch.

Kay McConnell is another dear friend always encouraging me in the long process.

Thank you, Kay McConnell.

I could mention so many others who helped me on this journey. However, the Great Healer, Great Teacher, and Dearest Friend who enabled me to do this is the greatest Father a girl could ever have; my forever Father, Jesus Christ.

Epilogue

On the way to Jerusalem, Jesus traveled along the border between Samaria and Galilee. As he was going to the village, ten men who had leprosy met him. They stood at a distance and called out in a loud voice,

> "Jesus, Master, have pity on us!"
> When he saw them, he said, "Go, show yourselves to the priests." And as they went, they were cleansed.
> One of them, when he saw he was healed, came back, praising God in a loud voice.
> He threw himself at the feet of Jesus. (Luke 17:11-19 NIV)

He was an outsider, a leper, a Samaritan who could not enter the temple. Not able to enter the temple but He knew another gate had opened for him. Jesus was the key that opened the gate.

He got healed while he was walking on the way.

The Damaged Child

He woke her up this morning
As she was sleeping there.
He saw a damaged child
That no one could repair.
Without his healing touch
She would not enjoy the sun
Or hear the singing of the birds.
Too much had gone wrong.
He opened her ears so she could hear
The singing of the doves.
He filled her soul with music.
He filled her heart with love.
He took her in his arms
As she was sleeping there.
He knew her wounded heart
No human could repair
Until she heard his voice one day
As she was walking on the waysz

CPSIA information can be obtained
at www.ICGtesting.com
Printed in the USA
BVHW060224021022
648341BV00001B/3